A PROFILE OF

HONG KONG

Library of Congress Cataloging-in-Publication Data on File

Hardcover: 9780825309496
Ebook: 9780825308536

For inquiries about volume orders, please contact:

Beaufort Books
27 West 2oth Street
Suite 1103
New York NY 10011
sales@beaufortbooks.com

Published in the United States by Beaufort Books
www.beaufortbooks.com

Distributed by Midpoint Trade Books,
a division of Independent Publishers Group
www.midpointtrade.com
www.ipgbook.com

Book Designed by Mark Karis

Printed in the United States of America

A PROFILE OF

HONG KONG

DURING TIMES PAST, TIMES CURRENT,
and ITS QUEST *of a* FUTURE
MAINTAINING HONG KONG'S LIBERTY

BRUCE HERSCHENSOHN

BEAUFORT
BOOKS

CONTENTS

BRUCE HERSCHENSOHN

1932-2020

Bruce's first book with Beaufort Books, *Above Empyrean*, was published in 2008. Following its release, we enjoyed a close working relationship with Bruce that spanned more than a decade and resulted in six exceptional works, including his sixth and final book, *A Profile of Hong Kong*.

When we first received Bruce's manuscript of *A Profile of Hong Kong*, Hong Kong was in the throes of years-long protests as the region's citizens fought for autonomy from China. With Bruce's frequent trips to Hong Kong over the course of his career, we had complete trust that he would bring respect, discernment, and expertise when telling Hong

Kong's turbulent story, and we were excited to bring such an important and timely dialogue into the national conversation.

Bruce was an old-school author who preferred working with a physical manuscript. Over the years, we gladly obliged, sending our notes, edits, and new drafts back-and-forth using nothing but the US Postal Service and a manila envelope. It was just after we sent the final manuscript of *A Profile of Hong Kong* to the designer that we learned of his passing. To honor Bruce's memory, and with his family's blessing, we decided to move forward with publishing *A Profile of Hong Kong* as is. Aside from light copyediting, the book you have before you is written in Bruce's signature style, the way Bruce would have wanted it published.

We will greatly miss Bruce, and we believe he would be thrilled to see his final book in the hands of discerning readers.

—ERIC KAMPMANN

A NOTE TO THE READER
FROM THE AUTHOR

A Profile of Hong Kong was adapted from previous books and articles and other media and forums in which I wrote or spoke about Hong Kong, including many travels to Hong Kong. Those travels became so frequent over the years that their regularity added up to approximately 37 annual trips to Hong Kong starting in 1960 through the 1997 handover of Hong Kong from Great Britain to the People's Republic of China. This book also records the beginning years in Hong Kong's history and goes into the new century's chapters of Hong Kong, including the frightening days and nights of 2019 and 2020.

1

LOOKING CENTURIES
BACK IN HONG KONG

[If you don't like reading about things that happened such a long time before your birth, don't read this chapter except for the last eight paragraphs, as those paragraphs of this chapter have a direct effect on the 21st Century to 2020.]

Abraham Lincoln was 32 years old practicing law in Springfield, Illinois when the history of Hong Kong began to have interest but not much. At the time, Hong Kong was one of the rarest major political entities on Earth that had a shorter known history than the United States. It's likely that Abraham Lincoln would have said that our country was threescore and five years old at the time Hong Kong's detailed history began if anyone had asked him. Fortunately, they didn't. He could save a revised version of a time-keeping line like that for later.

Although Lincoln didn't travel to Hong Kong, future visitors would be able to learn about the events and lives of Hong Kong people by asking those who had lived there. They talked of previous generations who passed on the events when Hong Kong Island off southern China had become nothing more than a camping ground for pirates and a place for transient fishermen who had either great courage or great ignorance to think it was a safe place. It was common to be told with many pieces of evidence that fishermen would often spend their last days in Hong Kong because pirates would slit the fishermen's throats for whatever possessions they carried and even for their catches of fish earlier in the day.

Those residents spoke of times they had lived through, as well as times their elders had lived through, prior to 1841. The history was passed down by residents as well as historians, many referring to British historical journals written far back that recorded that as many as 5,650 people were scattered in Hong Kong between villages and hamlets and boats.

There were two major and frequent biases that became obvious in foreign-born-authored history books of Hong Kong, dependent upon whether they had British or Chinese authors. Americans could now read a description of events based on those earlier people and books without any bias at all since American authors owed no instinctive allegiance to either Queen Victoria of Great Britain or the emperors of the Manchu Dynasty in China. The histories of the times that were written by the British did seem to have the most credibility since they were most meticulous and generally self-critical, while there were no self-criticisms in the histories written in China. (Perhaps that was true because China's public speakers and writers might have been frightened by their government's possible reaction to their work.)

Both powers were trading with each other, and it is apparent that both powers had superiority complexes. The British thought of the Chinese as unsophisticated, even uncivilized and primitive, devoted to ancient superstitions and myths, and the Chinese thought of the British as repugnant Europeans who were corrupt and filled with the ambition of exploitation and smelled of perfumes.

The Emperor dictated that the British (as well as any other Westerners) could trade only in a "trading season" and only in one small area of China within the factory area just outside of Canton, with the city of Canton itself being off-limits. The British were not allowed to bring their families into China but ordered to leave them in the Portuguese enclave of Macau, and the British traders were not allowed to learn or read or speak Chinese or to go out after dark. In both recorded histories, it doesn't seem like the British were having much fun.

To make things worse for the British of the time, the Chinese enjoyed a hefty trade imbalance since the Chinese had little interest or purchasing power for those things the British offered. That was not true for what the Chinese offered the British. The women of Great Britain had big eyes for Chinese jade and silks and porcelain, and both British women and men could not resist Chinese tea. In return for such British longings, the Chinese would accept nothing less than silver.

But Great Britain was not ready to surrender the trade imbalance to the Chinese. In a short time, they discovered there was one product many Chinese people wanted that the British *could* supply. The Emperor of China didn't want the product in his nations at all, but there were enough Chinese people who *did* want it:

Opium.

There was plenty of opium in the Bengal area of East India, which was a British colony. Not bad. Not good in obeying the law of the Emperor of China but not bad in obeying the law of supply and demand. The trade imbalance gradually shifted in that direction. It seemed as though the Chinese had a greater appetite for bad opium than the British had for good tea.

The Emperor of China was infuriated that opium addicts were replacing China's supply of silver. He appointed a Special Commissioner whose sole job was to stop the opium trade. He was Lin Tse-hsu, a name not worth remembering. He had a simple assignment, as all Lin had to do was cut off all food supplies to the British. The Chief Superintendent of British Trade in China, Charles Elliot, had a normal human reaction to Lin's solution. Charles Elliot became hungry. So did all his men. And so after six weeks of holding out and finally having run out of anything to eat, Charles Elliot produced the chests of opium that had been hidden from the Special Commissioner. Each chest weighed about 150 pounds. There were a lot of them. It was an embarrassment. There were 20,263 chests.

The Special Commissioner made a nighttime discovery of burning every one of the chests of opium and demanded the British get off Chinese territory.

They did. They went to Macau, but they didn't encounter a welcoming committee of resident natives. The Portuguese Governor of Macau said he couldn't be responsible for the safety of the British and that it would be best if they picked up their families they had previously left in Macau and have them go somewhere else.

But there was no land close by whose inhabitants would have them. So they went to ships that bounced around what today is Hong Kong Harbor until the unhappy trick that always works was imposed by the Chinese again. They call it the old Chinese Food-Cut-Off-Trick.

The Foreign Secretary of Great Britain, Lord Palmerston, was enraged at the treatment of the British traders. Lord Palmerston was what we would call a "hard-liner." He would have made Barry Goldwater in 1964 seem like a liberal softy. In retaliation for the treatment of the British, Lord Palmerston sent the British fleet to China and bombarded one city after another after another.

The Emperor's forces couldn't compete with the British who ruled the seas, and the Emperor appointed a negotiator named Qishan, whose name is also not worth remembering, who was forced to agree to the British that China would pay for the opium they had burned and allow the British traders back near Canton.

Britain's Chief Superintendent Charles Elliot was now in the driver's seat and said that wasn't enough, as he wanted a trade treaty or a good-sized island like Hainan where the British could camp permanently and bring their families and be safe. Qishan said there was no need for a trade agreement as the British could simply *have* Hong Kong Island (since at the time, Great Britain was the strongest of the nations in the world with some 62 colonies throughout the globe and sea-power exceeding all others).

And so, on the 26th of January 1841, the flag of Great Britain was unfurled on what became known as Possession Point of Hong Kong.

This treaty gave the British the territory of Hong Kong Island "in *perpetuity*"; that word meaning *forever*.

At the time, that agreement made no one happy. The Emperor was enraged at his negotiator for giving away one inch of Chinese territory and had Qishan brought to Peking in chains. [The name of Peking was generally still used until the late 1970s when the PRC transitioned into a new spelling and pronunciation for Chinese Mandarin into English called PINYIN in which, among many words, the capital city of Peking became Beijing. See "Glossary."]

And just like the Emperor of China was enraged at his negotiator for giving away Chinese territory and had brought Qishan to Peking in chains, Britain's Foreign Secretary Palmerston was just as angry at Elliot for accepting a deal that didn't give the British a trade treaty and only gave the British the crummy island of Hong Kong which Palmerston called "a barren island with hardly a house upon it."

As a result of all this, the Emperor of China banished Qishan to Tibet, and Britain's Foreign Secretary Palmerston sent Elliot to be Consul General in the Republic of Texas.

After that, Foreign Secretary Palmerston appointed a new commander, Sir Henry Pottinger, to take revenge on China. He did his job well. He blasted away at Canton, Xiamen, Ningbo, Shanghai, and threatened Nanking. This time the Emperor negotiated by himself or faced the risk of China being under British rule. He signed a trade treaty. Palmerston, who had previously demanded a better island than Hong Kong, had nothing more to say since his Whig government in London had fallen during all of this and the new Tory government had replaced him with a Foreign Secretary, Lord Aberdeen, who didn't care about possession of a small Chinese island.

Within five years, there was a population of over fifteen thousand people on Hong Kong Island, both Chinese and British, and practically all men. That's because there was only one career opportunity for women.

In 1847, there was a book published in London entitled *China* which had a chapter that told about the new possession of Great Britain from China. The chapter was called "Hong Kong—Its Position, Prospects, Character and Utter Worthlessness from Every Point of View to England."

Here the history gets murky. The Chinese took a British ship called *The Arrow* imprisoning the British crew, saying the ship was in their waters and it was loaded with pirates. The British history says it wasn't in their waters as it was registered in Hong Kong, and it had no pirates. Almost at the same time, the first British Envoy was en route to be the First Colonial Secretary of Hong Kong, and he was fired on by the Chinese on his way to Peking to present his credentials. With the Arrow incident and the shooting at the new British envoy, another was started.

At the conclusion of this war, the British secured diplomatic recognition by China and the British settled across the harbor from Hong Kong Island which now put them also on Kowloon after they secured that territory (with guns loaded), having argued that they were too isolated on an island alone and needed both sides of the harbor for safety with a military presence on the mainland.

Done. A new treaty. This one gave the British the tip of the Kowloon peninsula all the way to Boundary Street (not great territory) plus Stonecutters Island. (It's still called Stonecutters Island, although it isn't an island anymore since, by reclaimed land, it is now part of the mainland territory of Kowloon.) The new treaty gave the British this additional territory with the same definitive word by which China had given Great Britain Hong Kong

Island: *perpetuity*—meaning *forever*.

In summary, within the years between 1842-1898, three agreements in total were signed between China and Great Britain; two treaties—and one lease agreement.

First, there was the Treaty of Nanking signed in 1842, with China ceding Hong Kong Island in *perpetuity* (meaning *forever*) to Great Britain.

Second, in 1860, came signatures within the Convention of Peking, with another treaty; this one with China ceding Kowloon and Stonecutters Island in *perpetuity* (meaning *forever*) to Great Britain.

Third, there was the Second Convention of Peking in 1898. Not a treaty but an agreement with the New Territories was leased (not given—so *not* in perpetuity—*not* forever) to Great Britain for 99 years from the 1st of July 1898 projected to last through the 30th of June 1997. This time the Chinese said something like (the precise words were never recorded) "Okay, take it, but this time none of that perpetuity stuff anymore. We'll give you a lease, and we'll make it for 99 years and then you give back the new territory, since we'll all be dead by then anyway. You can have all the land up to the Sham Chun River for 99 years, and that's it."

Even without giving that territory to Britain and only giving a lease, the British accepted the offer. This parcel of land was called the New Territories, which was huge compared to what they had in Hong Kong and Kowloon. The New Territories, including 235 islands, were 92% of the total of all three entities. Since the agreement was signed in 1898 for 99 years, it meant the lease had a very distant deadline since it would likely be beyond their lives.

At the time, the British had no appetite for more than one Chinese name of British ownership of two territories and one lease, and that was probably why they called the whole collection of three territories (Hong Kong Island and Kowloon and the New Territories) by the single name of Hong Kong and that seemed to be acceptable worldwide. (Hong Kong means "Fragrant Harbor;" Kowloon means "Nine Dragons," one sacred Dragon for each of eight mountains in Kowloon plus one for the Emperor who, it was assumed, was also a Dragon; and the New Territories were the New Territories because that's what they were for the British.)

The New Territories required annual payments for which the British had to pay what was commensurate with 5,000 Hong Kong dollars a year, which was generally about 646 American dollars per year without indexing for inflation or opium. The British paid it, and the Chinese accepted the payments.

When the release of the New Territories took place, Franklin Delano Roosevelt was 16 years old. Throughout his life, he would remember the signing of the lease of the New Territories from China to Great Britain. He didn't like it. He was never high on colonialism. This had an indirect impact in years to come, but other events took precedence.

2

WARS

In summary, within the years between 1842 and 1898, when three agreements were signed between China and Great Britain, no agreement stopped the opium traffic. That traffic went on into the 1930s when China had a good deal more to worry about than either Great Britain or opium because of an immediate crisis: Japan attacked China in July of 1937.

No one appeared to leave China alone; this time uniquely. Germany, France, and Russia sent enforcements to *protect* China. It wasn't out of justice or compassion. They wanted "thank-you's" in trade and treaties and money from China. Great Britain was concerned that a terrible Europe versus Asia conflict was to break out, so they demanded more territory, not only to protect Hong Kong but now to protect China itself.

The 1937 attack from Japan on China included the taking of Nanking, Shanghai, and Peking. It was no contest, with Japan becoming the quick conqueror. This was the overture to the Asian theater of World War II.

The British Government of Hong Kong ordered thousands of their men to travel with their dependents to Australia for safety. Simultaneously, thousands of Chinese streamed into Hong Kong to be protected by its residents, both Chinese and British.

Then came the 7th of December 1941 (which was the 8th of December across the international Date Line in the Pacific Ocean, including in Hong Kong), when the Japanese Empire attacked Hawaii's Pearl Harbor, Malaysia, Singapore, and the Philippines, as well as invaded the British territory of Hong Kong, coming from the Chinese border of the New Territories and working their way southward. Prime Minister Winston Churchill gave the order for the British in Hong Kong to hold on. It was an impossible task, but the fight went on for eighteen days and nights through the New Territories, through Kowloon, and finally through Hong Kong Island.

On Christmas Day of 1941, the three entities of Hong Kong fell to Japan. Hong Kong's British Governor Mark Young had concealed himself in the Peninsula Hotel on

Kowloon, where the Japanese broke that concealment, found him, and sent him off to Manchuria as a prisoner.

The atrocities committed during the following three years and eight months are not only recorded well in books authored by victims and their relatives and witnesses in Hong Kong, but they are still discussed among some elderly who lived or were related to those in Hong Kong during those years. During that war, all subjects of Great Britain—other than the very old and ill—were imprisoned, the worst prison being in Sham Shui Po on Argyle Street in Kowloon. (Many years later, in the 1970s, the premises of the prison were destroyed and became a safeguard to house Vietnamese refugees. The entire area known as Sham Shui Po is now the most densely populated area in the world.)

Back to 1941, there then came one of the most incredible end-of-a-war stories ever to take place:

Arthur May, a British citizen, 34 years old, lived with his elderly and ill parents in Hong Kong. He knew that he was doomed to become a prisoner of the Japanese when Christmas Day of 1941 started, since the surrender of Hong Kong was imminent. In an act of sentiment and patriotism, he took the flag of Great Britain from an abandoned British campground, and he folded it neatly and hid it beneath a cushion of the couch in his parent's living room.

As he anticipated, he was taken off to prison. One of the fellow prisoners was Franklin Gimson, who had been the Number Two Man to Governor Young. Both men were inspirations to each other, with Gimson taking charge of the prisoners, continually giving them hope that the future would be theirs, and Arthur May acting in the service of Franklin Gimson. As the war entered its concluding year of 1945, Gimson and May had heard that President Roosevelt wanted Chiang Kai-shek of China to take Hong Kong when the war was done rather than having Hong Kong revert back to Great Britain. The United States was giving the orders in the Pacific Theater, and if that's what Roosevelt wanted, that is what Roosevelt would likely get at the end of the war.

But President Roosevelt died in April, and the war was still not done. President Truman didn't care whether colonialism survived or if it didn't survive. He said that when the war ended, as far as he was concerned, whichever of the two powers, Great Britain or China, would get to Hong Kong first could take it. After all, both Great Britain and China were allies of the United States in this war that would become known as World War II.

Of course, China had every advantage to get there first. China was just across the border, whereas Great Britain was across the globe. And so, Arthur May and Franklin Gimson devised a plan, a plan that as it worked out, did what even they could not have envisioned. Their act would save Hong Kong from 48 years of communist rule. This is what happened and how it happened:

Just before dawn of the 18th of August 1945, Arthur May escaped from his imprisonment along with a few others. Under his guidance, his small group went to his parents' home and rescued the flag that was placed beneath the couch cushion back on Christmas Day of 1941. Then they went on to Hong Kong Island's Victoria Peak, high above the city, where they raised the flag of Great Britain for all to see. Japanese soldiers rushed to them, but Arthur May told them Japan had surrendered and he was reclaiming the city for the Crown. The Japanese in Hong Kong didn't know what was true and what wasn't true, and the Japanese soldiers on the Peak were afraid that if they disallowed the flag to remain where Arthur May unfurled it, revenge would be taken on them by the British Government (if, indeed, the British Government was now in charge). When Franklin Gimson, at the prison camp, saw the distant flag above the Peak, he immediately took the oath of office as Acting Governor representing His Majesty King George VI, and he told the Japanese officers to get out of the prison encampment. With the same fear as the Japanese on the Peak, they obeyed.

It would take twelve more days until British ships could get to Hong Kong; twelve days that beyond any doubt could have brought the forces of China to simply cross the border and claim Hong Kong as theirs.

What no one could have known, not Arthur May or Franklin Gimson or King George VI or Chiang Kai-shek or President Truman, was that May and Gimson were saving Hong Kong from a fate that was even beyond the severity that they knew: Four years forward, in 1949, Chiang Kai-shek would lose the entire mainland of China to the communist rule of Mao Tse-tung, who would have included

Hong Kong as part of his captured territory from Chiang Kai-shek.

The flag of Arthur May saved Hong Kong for the British, at least for a time.

With the raising of that flag on Victoria Peak, the three agreements signed by Great Britain and China were back in effect as they were before the war. Franklin Gimson was soon *Sir* Franklin Gimson, and the Governor's Office was handed back to the freed prisoner, Governor Mark Young, and he resumed the Governorship he had begun before the Japanese attacked.

Had that flag not been saved and hidden on Christmas Day of 1941 and then raised almost four years later, the miracle of Hong Kong's triumph of freedom and free enterprise, including the most magnificent skyline in the world, would never have existed.

(During a Claremont Conference in Hong Kong, Arthur May was contacted through his closest friend, Jack Edwards, another historical figure who had been imprisoned by the Japanese in Singapore and Taiwan. Both still lived in Hong Kong. Arthur May was ill and confined to his bed, but he asked Jack Edwards to go to a session of the Claremont Conference with the flag that had saved Hong Kong. It was a moment no delegate to the Claremont Conference would ever forget. Listening to Jack Edwards was an inspirational hour, and for the conference attendees to touch that flag could only be compared to a careful, religious, exalted involvement.)

Before the decade of the 1950s ended, on the 1st of

October 1949, came the fall of China to Mao Tse-tung's communist government under which hundreds of thousands of escaped Chinese poured into Hong Kong, fleeing communist rule to live in the small British enclave. It was an influx then unparalleled in history.

Those who escaped to Hong Kong and Taiwan and to other friendly states were some of the survivors, while 47 million Chinese stayed in Mao's People's Republic of China, including those who became a part of the estimated 47-62 million Chinese who were killed by orders of Mao's government. [The numbers are from the U.S. and other nations, recognized human rights organizations, and even the lowest estimate of 47 million is a total that is more than Hitler's and Stalin's combined number of murders by orders of their government's leadership.]

Of course, prior to Mao's leadership, China was led by Chiang Kai-shek who was an ally of the western nations, including the U.S. and its allies in World War II. Chiang Kai-shek's China also became one of the five organizers at the start of the United Nations Organization, and therefore, the Republic of China became one of the five Permanent Members of the U.N. with all Permanent Members composing the U.N.'s Security Council. Then came Mao Tse-tung's leadership of China after winning that war over China's mainland from Chiang Kai-shek who escaped to Taiwan with many Chinese following him. Mao re-titled it to the *People's* Republic of China, which quickly became referred to as the PRC by Foreign Service Officers and many Heads of State and others (particularly by those who realized the people had nothing to do with Mao's new title he gave the nation of China, nor was his use of the word "republic" accurate because it surely was not being governed as a republic although that word had been used in the title before Mao's use of the word). Then the term "Red China" became frequently used by free governments and people.

Two other major wars were started in Asia before the end of the 1950s: the Korean War and the Vietnam War. The Korean War began in 1951, and with the U.N. embargo of goods from Communist China and the U.S. demanding a Certificate of Origin on any goods sold in Hong Kong to Americans (proving they were not manufactured in the People's Republic of China), Hong Kong pushed itself through great ambition and creativity to be a manufacturing center and exporter by producing and exporting electronics, including watches, clocks, and printing devices and engaging in clothing and many other light industries.

Just after 1960 started, the population of Hong Kong had swelled to three million—almost all refugees from China. They went, often by escape, to Hong Kong because Hong Kong would give them one gift that the People's Republic of China had not and would not deliver:

Liberty.

3

BUILDING MODERN
HONG KONG

The newer wars of Asia had started with North Korea invading South Korea and North Vietnam invading South Vietnam. (By the time 1960 began, the two Koreas had entered an Armistice Agreement which was not the end of the war but, in effect, was a temporary cease-fire while the Vietnam conflict was getting more and more intense.) Hong Kong was not directly involved with either war except that it was used as a willing place for Rest and Recreation of U.S. Troops and other allies when away from their assignment of aiding the defense efforts of South Korea and South Vietnam.

The 1960 skyline of Hong Kong Island was just beginning to achieve magnificence. Not all of it yet as in this year it still had clusters of colonial-style buildings and a few highrises with most other buildings capped with squatter-huts on their roofs. The harbor between Hong Kong Island and Kowloon was full of brown canvas junk boats with rickshaws supplying the land transportation on either side of the harbor.

To get across the harbor to either Kowloon from Hong Kong Island or to Hong Kong Island from Kowloon entailed the luxurious procedure of taking a Star Ferry, which endured its ecstasy-status by many Hong Kong people. That 1870's romantic relic remained the favored way to cross the harbor, still in that glorious voyage of seven minutes. Each ship was normally filled with passengers, one departure only minutes after another, and the announcement of a "thoughtless building of tunnels for auto traffic" caused concern of a coming slowdown in Star Ferry traffic with its old fleet of thirteen ships, each named after a star: Twinkling Star and Morning Star and Evening Star and Meridian Star and all kinds of stars.

The comforting, lasting familiarity of a Star Ferry was magnified by the uniqueness of the procedure: to walk down the concrete walkway and wait by the gated barrier until a small man in a dark blue uniform with white stripes on his sailor-style lapels opened the gateway, and the large warning-light above it turned from red to green. To be one of the first by the gateway was a loneliness that lasted no more than seconds as the lonely would be surrounded by waiting people and then would be swallowed by the pouring passengers as they passed the open gateway and down the ramp to the gangplank and onto the Star Ferry.

Each of the first ones aboard from Kowloon was expected, by tradition, to reverse the back of whatever long bench on which the oncoming passenger would decide to sit, so as to make all those who sat there face the direction of the destination. As soon as the passengers sat down and before the gate was closed, early morning men were already reading their *South China Morning Post* and *Hong Kong Standard* and dozens of newspapers in Chinese. And early morning women, dressed in brightly colored cheongsams with high collars and slit skirts, sat like proper and erotic Goddesses. All of this while it was only the morning. My God, what would later hours be like—not even to think of the nights. Other cities would writhe in jealousy if they knew what went on here off the South China Sea.

As passengers went through those comforting procedures known nowhere else on Earth, a loud bell rang to warn any more prospective passengers not yet aboard that soon the gateway would be closed, and the dark red gangplank would be raised, and they better run. Finally, there was the awkward rocking start of the forward motion with the accompanying noise of water lapping against the wooden hull of the Star Ferry. Then, from Kowloon, Hong Kong Island started to come closer, getting larger and larger and larger.

The only awkward, out-of-context interruption of this

magnificent, short journey was a sign that read, "Do Not Spit. Beware of Pickpockets." The warning seemed to be effective. Generally, no one spit, and at least no one could be seen picking anyone's pocket.

The ride was all too quick. One of the small men in the deep-blue uniform put on his thick, dirty, worn gloves and heaved the ship's rope and there was a bump of the ship, and its motors stopped, and there was the boat's uneven swaying as it started being pulled towards the Hong Kong Island side of the harbor. As the rope was being wrapped around the protruding cleat of iron on the dock, the passengers rose, rushing to stand in mass by the small man in the uniform who was waiting for the signal that the boat would stop hitting the side of the dock so he could free the gangplank barrier and lower it. When it was lowered, the crowd poured out like a torrent of freed water, heading up the walkway to a myriad of destinations.

On a mid-October day of 1960, twelve traveling Americans made an invited journey to the U.S. Consulate of Hong Kong; the journey called for a Star Ferry ride if coming from Kowloon, and no matter from where the guest was coming, to get to the Consulate meant going to the Hong Kong Island side of the harbor, then a short walk up to the 26 Garden Road entrance to the U.S. Consular Offices.

After being greeted by the Consul General and the Public Affairs Office, the twelve guests were seated around a conference table and given coffee and cookies to eat and greetings to the U.S. Consulate in Hong Kong, including a question and answer session that became filled with prophecy of what would happen in the "coming handover" of Hong Kong to the People's Republic of China scheduled for the 1st of July 1997. That was followed by each guest receiving Xeroxed copies of two newspaper columns; both from the *Hong Kong Standard* with the dates of April 27, 1960 and September 21, 1960, from which the following are excerpted as below:

> "We could allow it (1997) to worry us into hysteria; we could let it convince us that it is futile to work and live, we could fold our hands now and wait for the takeover 37 years hence.

> "But how would such a course of action help? If we tormented ourselves into worries of 1997, it would merely make us less capable of tackling the real problems of the day and more vulnerable to Red China's threats and demands.

> "Being incapable of averting the inevitable, Hong Kong has no choice but to continue to live on the premise that in the changeableness of the situation on the mainland, a lot can happen in 37 years...

> "Although the debate on constitutional reform has been going on in the colony for a considerable period of time, public thinking on the question still seems to be clouded and uncertain...This may in part be attributed to the fact that opponents of reform continue to advance the same old arguments which have obscured and confused the issues since the beginning.

"One of these is the assertion that there is no need for reform because there is at present no loud public demand for it. But the absence of such a demand cannot be construed to mean that it is not required.

"Experience in many parts of the world has shown vividly and unmistakably that, by the time popular demand becomes impassioned and strident, it is much too late to carry out such reform quietly and peacefully. The question we must ask ourselves is, will such a violent demand arise in the future, if nothing is done now?...

"Of course, Hong Kong is not ready for full self-government at this moment. But this does not mean that measures should not be undertaken now to prepare the population for the future. One might just as well hold that because it would be dangerous to have a person who knows nothing about cars suddenly put at the wheel of a car in our downtown traffic. That person should not be permitted to drive."

What that meant is that the Governors of Hong Kong representing the Crown from 1843 forward did little, if anything, to bring about self-government. Certainly, the laws of British authoritarianism were still on the books, but they were neither used nor abused by Great Britain. Still, they probably should have been removed from those books rather than be part of the booty of a post-1997 government that may well want to have such an inheritance of authoritarian laws. (In the following year, the Hong Kong Journalists Association pinpointed seventeen such authoritarian laws.) It should be known, however, that since the time Hong Kong became a British colony, with little exception, the people of Hong Kong didn't demand or even appeal for democracy prior to 1960, nor even to some later years, because they had been given by the British a safe refuge in their escape from the People's Republic of China. They knew that most nations did not offer such freedom within refuge. And for most Hong Kong people, liberty under the British was so good, with no pressing need for new law books and self-government. Further, they were grateful to the British for ignoring all the authoritarianism that they could have raised by taking away their God-given freedoms—and that so many other powers might well have devastated. It was also known that a succession of United States Governments would and did endorse the freedoms given to Hong Kong people by the British Government of Hong Kong. (Note the expression of "Hong Kong people" was invented and is most widely used by Hong Kong people with great pride as their definition of their new heritage or home territory. While it is rare to hear some resident of one or another country attach the word "people" to explain their heritage or derivation, the residents called themselves "Hong Kong people" while no one from Finland or Mexico would likely say, "I am a Finland person" or "I am a Mexico person." If you don't think this point is valid, then that's too bad.)

The moment an international airliner landed and the doors opened on the soil of Hong Kong, the outgoing passengers inhaled the unique and intoxicating fragrance of that city. The inhalations were deep, and instead of receiving a penalty for intoxication, there was a reward of a totally non-harmful, legal, and very pleasant breathing pattern that was the introduction to what was becoming the most magnificent city in the world.

The increasing modernization was turned into realization on a huge scale by the creativity and abilities of the Hong Kong people. It would not take long before there was a skyline on Hong Kong Island unlike any other skyline in the world. Buildings were reaching into the clouds, with each new tower built totally different from any neighboring building. A new building that could only have been designed by Howard Roark in *The Fountainhead* would stand next to a building that even Roark wouldn't have had the imagination to design. Annual visits to Hong Kong would be too infrequent to keep up with the changes in the architectural fantasy. At night, some buildings appeared to have had Walt Disney as the architect of colors and light patterns, and the beams of lights that bounced from each of the high-rises were of brilliant, varied colors and lengths of time before those lights changed colors. There would also be their reflections in the harbor waters between Hong Kong Island and Kowloon. (Kowloon was not permitted such brilliant or blinking or flashing night lights as such a galaxy was judged to be too dangerous for night-time landings or airliners as they approached for landings at the one airport, Kai Tak Airport on Kowloon, that was serving all three territories of Hong Kong Island, Kowloon, and the New Territories. Its location on Kowloon meant pilots stressed their ability to land without making the airliner travel too dangerously between buildings.)

As Hong Kong became more and more matchless, it became a city of fast-paced Hong Kong people frequently running to one place from another, and of confused and joyful tourists who seemed bewildered as they held tight to road maps and tour books and were not walking but running between massive shopping malls, stupendous hotels, and outdoor salespeople that sold unnecessary but terrific things.

In contrast, there were luxuries of Hong Kong, such as reserving tea-time seats at the Peninsula Hotel in Kowloon, and on Hong Kong Island, going up the Peak Tram all the way from its entrance on the level ground across the street from the Hilton Hotel, all the way to the top of the Peak, and while on that trip watching through the windows to see the buildings that passed appear to be falling; an illusion from the tram's tracks that were tilted up the mountain and the tram could do nothing to level it off.

Back on level land, with frequency, there were religious shrines seemingly of all faiths, and separate and apart from them were statues of every known religious figure imaginable, including a wonderful cluster of what appears to be a zillion Buddhas. The frequent, sacred structures put the crowded city into a valuable perspective.

In the 1960s, Hong Kong was becoming one of the great destinations for world travelers. While many of those world travelers would find out that some of the visited cities have characteristics of other cities they had visited, Hong Kong didn't do such a thing. It didn't look, sound, taste, feel, or have the aroma of any other city. And there was something else that was unique, and that fact would become known only after the traveler returned home:

Unlike most great cities in the world, once you have visited Hong Kong, it would never stop visiting you.

4

THE CULTURAL
REVOLUTION OF 1966-1976

The 1960s of modernization in Hong Kong was not going to cover the entire decade all the way to its end. In 1966, the Cultural Revolution of Mao Tse-tung began in China, and in 1967 came the interruption in Hong Kong *from* the Cultural Revolution. Red Guards from China, with a militia of 300 Chinese soldiers, crossed the border into Hong Kong territory while wearing wide red bands on their left arms and with their right hands, they were waving little red books above their heads, and they were carrying automatic rifles on their shoulders.

There were riots in Hong Kong staged by those soldiers and by others who supported Mao Tse-tung. The rioters were harmful but not successful in any long sense against Hong Kong people and the British Government. Additionally, in case of emergency, on orders from the Crown, the British Government, along with the Hong Kong Police, had put together quick emergency plans that included an aircraft on alert at Kai Tak Airport for Governor David Trench and his family, constantly ready to take him and his family to safety should the Red Guards take over targets in Hong Kong. The same was done for any other obvious targets.

On a much lesser scale were largely wide economic repercussions, as toward the end of 1967, the British Pound Sterling was devalued in Great Britain, with Hong Kong losing one-third of its sterling reserves. All of this paled in importance to the danger possible to befall Hong Kong residents and what tortures already befell those Chinese who, in China, would not wave Little Red Books in visual support of their nation's leader, Mao Tse-tung. Maybe Mao Tse-tung had gone crazy, but could so many Chinese people have also lost their sanity in the killing of their own neighbors? That neighborhood was the entire mainland of China, with an estimated two million tortured and killed within this Cultural Revolution.

To make a public statement of Mao Tse-tung's government by his People's Republic of China against the British jurisdiction of Hong Kong, the British Embassy in Peking was ransacked, and then most of the Embassy was destroyed by those who were Red Guards. Mao Tse-tung ordered all of China's food shipments to Hong Kong stopped. Hong Kong's major water supply from China was turned off, causing Hong Kong citizens to have no more than four hours of water from the tap every four days.

On the streets of Kowloon, mobs of students who supported the Red Guards stoned Europeans and Americans, and some buildings were set on fire. American naval personnel were sent back to their ships. Government House was surrounded by a mass of young students demonstrating their sympathy with the Cultural Revolution, singing "Unity is Strength" as they claimed they were members of the "Committee for Resisting British Oppression" and calling for an end to British "fascist atrocities."

It was almost two o'clock in the morning outside Hong Kong's Tsim Sha Tsui Train Station where a young lady was sitting in the backseat of a car, a driver keeping the motor running, both passenger and driver nervously looking at the doorway for the appearance of her parents, hoping no mobs of Red Guard supporters would charge the place. The driver of the car and the whole scheme of the evening had been arranged by friends recommended by a daring man who had walked in escape from the People's Republic of China. The journey of her parents from Canton in China, for which they had planned for months, was scheduled to reach the train station within a few dangerous hours. But the long-planned objective had been cut in half. The rescue of their parents had become the rescue of the mother alone.

Since their father was a mathematics teacher, and teachers were considered by the Red Guards of the Cultural Revolution to be "revisionists" to be exterminated, in March, he had been forced to kneel on broken glass and "confess his crimes." And then, unable to lift himself, he was lifted up by students, a wooden board was locked around his neck, a white dunce cap was put on his head, and he was paraded for two hours through the streets of Kwangchow while crowds threw rocks at him on the way to his execution.

The principal of the school in which the young girl's father had taught had been beaten on a daily basis by students, and when the beatings became intolerable, he killed himself.

All this had started on the 16th of May of the preceding year, 1966, when Mao Tse-tung created his new revolution with his wife Jiang Qing, designated as the Supreme Commander. The adult citizens of China were ordered to report their thoughts to students twice a day, and it was demanded that the adults had to participate in daily "Loyalty Dances." The objective of Mao's revolution was to be "closer to the masses than any leader in world history," by eliminating all those who existed between him and the people, which meant the persecution of those in the government itself, including State President Liu Shaoqi, and all teachers, academics, and artists. Most schools were closed, and teachers were condemned, bureaucrats were accused of taking too much authority from the people, and beating them to death was encouraged. All students were told to be

Red Guards and bring about the Cultural Revolution with Mao as their one and only father.

That mother was told that her husband had been buried, which was considered to be a kind gesture of the Red Guards since, in comparison, in Kwangsi-Chuang, over one hundred people were cannibalized, their organs boiled and served in cafeterias by the Red Guards. Still, her mother had to pay for the bullet used to kill her father.

All of this was accompanied by the apprehension of many Hong Kong residents and by those Chinese who, in China, would not wave Little Red Books in visual support of their nation's leader, Mao Tse-tung.

Shortly, because of the Cultural Revolution and all its demands, there were more and more escapes from Chinese residents, causing a pouring over the border from the People's Republic of China into Hong Kong through the New Territories, Kowloon, and Hong Kong Island.

The Cultural Revolution was officially done. But not completely done because the horror of it would be felt for generations to come, mainly because of the vacancy of those gone from life by means of that dictatorial pursuit by the government of the People's Republic of China.

5

MARGARET THATCHER
VS. DENG XIAOPING

In the decade ahead, the increase in population of Hong Kong became even larger from the 1975 victory of North Vietnam over South Vietnam, because now some 57,000 Vietnamese refugees started pouring into Hong Kong on makeshift boats, and they were readily accepted by Hong Kong as their destination of first refuge. (20,000 remained in camps of Hong Kong rather than face any possibility of repatriation into Vietnam.) The Hong Kong Government was faced with the suicides of some refugees who somehow feared they would have to go back to Vietnam. There was also fear of having to go to the People's Republic of China, as the PRC demanded that all Vietnamese refugees be out of Hong Kong by the time of their anticipated and certain takeover of Hong Kong on July 1, 1997.

The calendar was moving fast, and in 1982, Great Britain's Prime Minister Margaret Thatcher felt the time was right to meet with the leader of the People's Republic of China, Deng Xiaoping. The reason she felt the time was right was that she now had a world-known position of military strength coming from her Navy's victory against Argentina in the short Falkland Islands War that gave proof of the current power of Great Britain. This fact was combined with a tough necessity from something concerning the due date of the PRC takeover of the New Territories, because mortgages in the New Territories covered fifteen-year spans, and fifteen years from 1982 was 1997, the year the lease of the New Territories was over. No leases had been granted covering any dates beyond the 27th of June 1997, three days prior to the scheduled takeover of those New Territories by the People's Republic of China. Prime Minister Thatcher felt that a conversation with Deng Xiaoping should not be left undone any longer.

She met with him in Beijing on the 24th of September 1982, which was the first time a British Prime Minister had ever been in China. Not all of the precise dialogue was made public, but the overall positions were publicly released. Prime Minister Thatcher's position was that Hong Kong

Island and Kowloon were the property of Great Britain in perpetuity by virtue of the two treaties in which China ceded those lands to Great Britain in perpetuity. But, of course, the other agreement—the 99-year lease on the New Territories should now be discussed as Prime Minister Thatcher wanted it extended for another 99 years. It was also clear that without the New Territories, Hong Kong would have a tough time being totally self-reliant. Almost 40 percent of the residents lived in the New Territories, and it was 92 percent of all the three entities combined of what the world knew as Hong Kong.

She discovered that Deng Xiaoping's position was that the three agreements were "unequal" (according to the translator, meaning to him that the three agreements were signed under duress.) Deng's Foreign Office released the statement, "Hong Kong is part of Chinese territory. The treaties concerning the Hong Kong area between the British Government and the Government of the Manchu Dynasty of China were unequal treaties that have never been accepted by the Chinese people. The consistent position of the Government of the People's Republic of China is not bound by these unequal treaties and that the whole of Hong Kong area will be recovered when conditions are ripe."

Prime Minister Thatcher responded that "If a country will not stand by one treaty, it will not stand by another," and that abrogating that perpetuity clauses of two of the three agreements would be "very serious indeed."

Deng was not moved to change his mind.

The 1st of July 1997 would be the date that all three agreements would be changed to the territories of the People's Republic of China. He had one major factor on his side in that China was just across a land border from what he was claiming while Great Britain was across the globe (and no longer a feared colonial power—no matter the recent Falklands victory.)

Prime Minister Thatcher took her British plane from Beijing to Hong Kong, where she told the Hong Kong people that Great Britain had a "moral responsibility" to Hong Kong and that Great Britain took that responsibility "very, very seriously."

A new poll was then taken of Hong Kong people with 95 percent of the respondents wanting the political status-quo of Hong Kong under the British totally maintained.

In the past, demonstrations were virtually absent throughout Britain's government of those three territories, but the great mass of Hong Kong people had not been thinking seriously long ahead until "long ahead" was on a visible horizon. Now the calendar dictated that it was on a visible horizon.

Now two years of negotiations began by the representatives of both leaders.

Those negotiations went Deng's way.

Almost two years to the day, on the 26 of September 1984, the Joint Declaration between Great Britain and the People's Republic of China was released. There was not to be a new 99-year lease of the New Territories as Prime Minister

Thatcher wanted. The whole of Hong Kong, meaning Hong Kong Island, Kowloon, and the New Territories would be turned over to the People's Republic of China when the lease on the New Territories would run out. Instead of Great Britain retaining Hong Kong and Kowloon in perpetuity while negotiating a new lease on the New Territories, the Joint Declaration was calling for the People's Republic of China to take over all three entities on July 1, 1997, with those three entities under "one country, two systems," with Hong Kong, Kowloon, and the New Territories going to the ownership of the People's Republic of China but still able to retain their system for fifty years, until the year 2047. This meant that the time period of 1997-2047 would see all three territories be used as a Special Administrative Region (SAR) of the People's Republic of China.

Hong Kong was an unhappy place. And the friends of Hong Kong became more pessimistic about Hong Kong's fate, because not only was it a terrible demand of Deng Xiaoping, but his government of the People's Republic of China was not noted for keeping its leader's word, even to its own citizens.

The Joint Declaration was filled with guaranteeing language, including guarantees for the people of Hong Kong during the period of the SAR that the "rights and freedoms, including those of the person, of speech, of the press, of assembly, of association, of travel, of movement, of correspondence, of strike, of choice of occupation, of academic research, and of religious belief, will be ensured by law…"

But the Constitution of the People's Republic of China already gives nearly all the same guarantees to its own people, and those guarantees are not observed. Article 35 of the Constitution of the People's Republic of China states: "Citizens of the People's Republic of China enjoy freedom of speech, of the press, of assembly, of association, of procession, and of demonstration." Article 36 guarantees "freedom of religious belief." Article 34 gives the right to vote and stand for election. None of it means anything.

(These kinds of guarantees are not uncommon in constitutions of communist societies. Article 34 in the Constitution of the former Soviet Union stated: "Citizens of the USSR are equal before the law, without distinction of origin, social or property status, race or nationality, sex, education, language, attitude to religion, type and nature of occupation, domicile, or other status. The equal rights of citizens of the USSR are guaranteed in all fields of economic, political, social, and cultural life." Article 49 stated that "persecution for criticism is prohibited" and Article 50 guaranteed "freedom of speech, of the press, and of assembly, meetings, street processions, and demonstrations." In most, if not all communist documents, there are caveats, but with or without them, communist societies have simply done those things they wanted to do at the time they wanted to do them.)

Many Hong Kong people felt betrayed by Great Britain and were especially resentful that Hong Kong people were given no voice in the negotiations. But they knew, and some admitted, that the People's Republic of China held all the cards geographically as well as militarily, and also in terms of much water and food supplied to Hong Kong by China. All of that while Prime Minister Thatcher had no such similar threats to give the PRC.

Other than democracy activists who were led by what would become familiar names of Martin Lee Chu-ming and Szeto Wah, and others perhaps not as visible as those two, felt they must simply accept the fate they were being dealt—and maybe there would somehow come some miracle. There was no question that the great majority of Hong Kong wanted Great Britain to stay and continue its jurisdiction of all three territories.

213 years earlier, on the 18th of April 1775, Paul Revere gave the call no one wanted to hear in the United States: "The British are coming! The British are coming!" On the 26th of September 1984, the call that caused fear in Hong Kong was, "The British are leaving! The British are leaving!"

6

HONG KONG PEOPLE IN PUBLIC DEMONSTRATIONS OF PROTEST

The Government of Great Britain received more hostility and blame from Hong Kong People for the coming 1997 takeover by the People's Republic of China than Great Britain had ever before endured from Hong Kong people.

London knew the Chinese were looking over the shoulders of their Governors of Hong Kong, and unfortunately, the British didn't want to cause the Chinese Government apprehensions that could be avoided, so Governors remained silent. And it must be admitted that even if the British had given democracy to Hong Kong as soon as they planted their flag back in 1841, there is no reason to believe the People's Republic of China would observe democracy in Hong Kong after the coming takeover. Similarly, if Great Britain had rid their law books of any authoritarian ability, there is no reason to believe it would make any difference once the Union Jack would come down the flagpole at the Government House at the midnight that cuts the 30th of June from the 1st of July 1997.

There was another element behind the more recent hostility leveled by Hong Kong people against the British: there was no threat coming from the British to those who dressed them down. No untoward consequences would come to those who would swear at the British. Consequences would, however, likely come to those who might want to curse the People's Republic of China after the 30th of June 1997. For Hong Kong people, there were not endless periods of time to be angry at their government, and this might be one of the last opportunities to employ such dissent with safety.

Just before Christmas of 1988, there was a demonstration close to the Star Ferry Pier on the Hong Kong side. Nothing like this demonstration had ever occurred against the British Government by Hong Kong People.

All the posters and placards that the demonstrators carried by the Star Ferry Pier were hand-made. Some of the crowd yelled out chants.

Some of the posters and chants were as follows:

"Sir David Ford-the dear Chief Secretary—While you and your British buddies can wave 'bye-bye' to Hong Kong in 1997 or earlier, returning to your London homes to enjoy more 'fish and chips and tea,' we, and our sons and daughters, and theirs, are going to remain in our Hong Kong homes. Therefore, if you cannot support us nor are concerned about Hong Kong people's struggle for democracy and freedom after 1997, would you please stop making stupid statements and shut up when you have nothing to say? We, the great Hong Kong people, will be accountable and responsible to the history of Hong Kong, our home!"

"The future of five and one half million Hong Kong people is not in the USA, Canada, Australia, New Zealand, and other immigration havens, but right where we are."

"The two hottest collector's items in Hong Kong after 1997 are democracy and freedom. Have you saved some for your children yet? If you don't support democracy and freedom now, can you look your children and your grandchildren in their faces later, knowing you could have done something now, however small?"

"Tea and Sympathy? Have tea, Sir David, but where's your sympathy for Hong Kong people?"

The major validity of any of the criticism against the British colonialists came from the fact that Great Britain did not establish democracy published in Hong Kong decades ago, and had it done so, when the turnover would come in 1997, there would already be a long-standing printed establishment of democracy—maybe.

7

1997 ARRIVING EARLY

PASSPORTS

The passport that had been used by traveling citizens of Hong Kong had been the British Dependent Territories Citizen (BDTC) passport. But July 1, 1997 would now become the date those passports would no longer be part of a British dependent territory.

Therefore, Great Britain established a British National (Overseas) passport (BNO) for those who had the British Dependent Territories Citizen passport. Being issued in a phase-in program by age groups with cut-off times for each age group, 1,023,244 Hong Kong people applied for and were issued those new passports in 1993 alone. The objective of the British Government was to distribute all those requested by the 1st of July 1997 when British Dependent Territories Citizen passports would become nothing more than pieces of nostalgia. In the period of time from the current to the 1st of July 1997, Hong Kong people were allowed to hold both styles of passports, but neither one allowed residency for Hong Kong people in Great Britain. The question became, of what value would the new passports have after the 1st of July 1997.

The answer was souvenirs. At best, those passports might be able to act as travel documents, but since Great Britain was not willing to have them be valid for the "right of abode" (ability to live) in Great Britain, they could well become no more than expensive relics of transition. The People's Republic of China had already designed and displayed its SAR Passport for distribution after the 30th of June 1997.

Without the right of abode, the quest for foreign passports permitting residency elsewhere began, and with that quest was a simultaneous hostility directed against Great Britain for, as some democracy advocates put it, "creating a document without regard to Right or Wrong but rather with regard to White or Wong."

CURRENCY

More and more of the coins in the pocket of Hong Kong people had rushed a picture of a Bauhinia flower rather than the familiar picture of Queen Elizabeth as it used to be. A picture of that Bauhinia seemed to be everywhere in Hong Kong and would be the predominant part of Hong Kong's new flag, with a white five-petal Bauhinia having a red star on each petal with the whole petal resting against a revolutionary red background. Some coins would be coming with a picture of Deng Xiaoping and, ominously with a picture of Tiananmen Square. It was expected that street names would be changed from commemorating British Governors and other British personalities. "Queen's Road," may well not last much beyond June of 1997. It was feared that Hong Kong itself may become known as Xiang Gang.

PRODUCTS FOR SALE

"Rice Paddy Babies," teddy-bear-like dolls that used to be sold throughout Hong Kong, became difficult to find. Each Rice Paddy Baby wore a necklace with a miniature British passport attached, asking the potential buyer to take the particular Rice Paddy Baby out of Hong Kong before 1997.

MEDIA

Some of the changes already apparent or sure to come were to be expected, while others were more frightening, particularly the self-censorship of some in the press.

Larry Feign, the anti-PRC cartoonist who authored and drew the comic strip, *The World of Lily Wong* published for eight years in the *South China Morning Post*, was out of a job. The publisher said he was let go because of "budgetary reasons." Maybe. Feign responded, "Self-censorship in the

Hong Kong media seems to be an AIDS-like virus that is spreading rapidly and for which there is no cure."

When the motion picture documentary *Mainland China 1989*, was screened in Hong Kong art theater, 17 minutes from the 78-minute film were missing. Deleted were interviews with mainland dissidents and pro-democracy leaders. It was said that the cuts were not to protect those who made the cuts, but officials said that without the cuts, the film "could seriously damage our relations with other countries."

Hong Kong reporter Xi Yang was seized while visiting Beijing for his mother's funeral, then tried and sentenced to 12 years imprisonment for disclosing to his Hong Kong newspaper, *Ming Pao*, that the PRC planned to meet its debts by selling gold. The PRC charged that he stole state secrets.

Chan Ya was a columnist for Hong Kong's *Express Daily News*, who wrote a column in support of the imprisoned Xi Yang. Chen Ya's column was discontinued.

Jimmy Lai, Hong Kong publisher of the magazine *Next*, was punished for his anti-PRC articles by the PRC closing down the Beijing branch of his Giordano store until he resigned as company chairman.

When the newspaper, *The Eastern Express*, was inaugurated in 1994 with critical coverage of the People's Republic of China, Huang Xinhua of the Chinese Communist Party declared that Hong Kong journalists "should be wise" and "act in line with the circumstances. Take these words to C.K. Ma (the owner of *The Eastern Express*) and tell him to watch out."

An unintimidated Hong Kong Magazine, *Contemporary*, reported that the PRC Government "collects files on reporters and separates newspapers into four categories, including a bottom group that should be isolated and attacked."

Some Hong Kong journalists who were once critical of Beijing now bent over backwards to refrain from criticism, while some who continued to write articles critical of Beijing were using pen names.

There was a weekly magazine available in Hong Kong and on some newsstands around the world called *Window*, which was a PRC view of "Hong Kong today." An editorial by Gerald Chen gave an insight to the press in the U.S. that was widely recognized as the most developed and respected in the world. But it is not difficult to see that such freedom would not work in Hong Kong under either the British or Chinese rule. A learned columnist commented: "It could turn very undesirable, unsustainable, and incompatible if (the U.S.-style of press freedom) was transplanted to Hong Kong...it could be found to be too free, too permissive, and too intrusive. It is like food that is too rich and possibly indigestible for some people...One can imagine what social turmoil would ensue if Hong Kong's media were to bring out the skeletons in the closets of public figures such as members of the Legislative and Executive Councils. As for the public's right to know, the trial of O.J. Simpson, the U.S. football hero, for the double murder of his ex-wife Brown Nicole (sic) and her friend Ronald Clark (sic) provides food for thought."

Against this background, a Claremont Conference on

"The Future of Hong Kong" invited three leading Hong Kong journalists to discuss with the delegates the atmosphere surrounding the Hong Kong media.

The journalists were Frank Ching = Senior Editor of the *Far Eastern Economic Review*; George Shen = Chief Editor of the *Hong Kong Economic Journal*; and Jesse Wong = the Hong Kong Bureau Chief of the *Asian Wall Street Journal*. It is accurate to say that each of the three journalists exhibited friendship and admiration for one another but did not necessarily agree with every statement. Some of the more pertinent thoughts follow:

> "It is known that the Chinese authorities located here in the Chinese News Agency Xinhua keep files on journalists and there is some concern that people will be taken to task after 1997 for what they have written. So, there is some self-censorship. But it is awfully difficult to get evidence of this because no one is going to tell you that 'I thought this, but I wrote something else.' But there is evidence that censorship is coming from management of some publications."

> "Within Hong Kong, there are two television stations. Both practice self-censorship...One of them has had the life of Mao for over a year and still has not shown it. The station insists that it just hasn't scheduled it yet."

> "There may be changes in establishing new bureaus in Hong Kong after the 1st of July 1997. News bureaus

that locate on the mainland must get permission from China's Foreign News Agency. Whether this will be true in Hong Kong after 1997 is unknown now."

"Some newspapers are now investing in China. That has great implications."

"Very often reporters have very different views than their editors. I don't know if editors will interfere."

"I do not think the Chinese leaders will be so foolish as to kill Hong Kong's press freedom. The free flow of information must continue, or the market is dead, and if the market is dead, Hong Kong is dead. But when you think of the track record of China and of their thinking up north, some people say that one country, two systems will result in the local communists being the greatest threat—much greater than Beijing. The PLA (the People's Liberation Army) will not march into my office, but local communists may like to make sure that what they perceive as troublemakers do not make too much trouble."

"Press freedom is one thing that is not given to you; it is your own right, so why take it from yourself."

"What's going to happen? Will it be worse or better? Hong Kong's press under the British can do virtually anything it wants, so there is reason to believe there will be less freedom, not more. China's press has no freedom. The People's Republic Foreign Ministry said, 'Of course it will be free, but it should be pro-Hong Kong and patriotic.' They use qualifiers. They all use qualifiers. They are not the first officials to say one thing and then render it meaningless by a list of qualifiers."

"Yes, Larry Feign (the anti-PRC cartoonist) had to leave the *South China Morning Post* but ten percent of the staff had to leave at that time, so I believe it was for economic reasons. I see no difference now in the *South China Morning Post.*"

"In the Chinese language newspapers in Hong Kong people read not only the news, but page after page of daily columns written by all different people and they write about all kinds of things; sometimes political elements, where people look for clues. More blatant political news is what we call 'Box-office Poison,' but readers all go for these small columns for clues."

"When I was in the U.S. for a month recently, I read the *New York Times* and the *Washington Post* every day and saw perhaps one article on Hong Kong. They don't cover Hong Kong all that much."

"There are publications right now that cannot get advertisers from corporations doing business on the mainland. Their ads must go through a number of official agencies in China. But that is the exception, not the rule."

"Revenue from advertising can suffer if the publication takes a position against the PRC. Beijing simply tells advertisers not to advertise."

"I hear all the talk and the fears about the outlook for the press, but I am optimistic."

In short time, all Hong Kong reporters were issued a warning by the PRC with Zhang Junsheng, Deputy Director at Xinhua, saying that Hong Kong reporters should familiarize themselves with Chinese laws and culture "to avoid trouble." He said that Deng Xiaoping's three principles of patriotism are to "respect one's own race, support Hong Kong's return to the motherland, and maintain Hong Kong's prosperity."

DISCUSSION OF THE PRC

The daughter of Deng Xiaoping had said that her father would be in Hong Kong for the midnight takeover of Hong Kong to his government even if he had to be there in a wheelchair. (The whispered joke in Hong Kong was that he was already dead, but everybody was afraid to tell him.) There are very few who can quite figure out how the government of the People's Republic of China works as it has no parallel elsewhere in the world, nor is there a prescribed orderly transition of leadership. Deng himself, in late offices, held only one position: The Chairman of the Bridge Commission, which did not deal with bridges over rivers but rather dealt with the game of bridge. Despite a lack of any other official position, Deng Xiaoping was known as the "Paramount Leader" of the People's Republic of China. (After much searching, I have been unable to find any other Bridge Commissioner who is the Paramount Leader of any other country.)

Every Chinese leader from the beginning of the communist revolution forward from Mao Tse-tung, Chou En-Lai, Deng Xiaoping, Li Peng, and Jiang Zemin had said the same sentence with repetitious precision: "By the end of this century, all Chinese territory will be back in the embrace of the motherland." The "embrace" will come to Hong Kong on the 1st of July 1997, Macau on the 20th of December 1999. The Spratly Islands are being "embraced" one by one, including the establishment of military enclaves, and the sovereignty of the entire South China Sea is being claimed by the People's Republic of China.

The crown jewel, Taiwan, remains continually threatened as a "renegade province" and is totally perceived by the People's Republic of China as an integral part of "the motherland" to be "embraced."

8

THE LANGUAGE OF LIBERTY: TWO GIANT HONG KONG PEOPLE

Martin Lee Chu-Ming, being one of the two most prominent Hong Kong people of his time, was in the Legislative Council from 1985 to 1997 at the seconds before the takeover by China. He not only believes in liberty for the people of Hong Kong, although that is obviously his first passion, but he has a belief in liberty for people all over the world. He was one of the Hong Kong leaders who demanded from the British

Government in Hong Kong that each Vietnamese refugee in Hong Kong must be given the highest humane treatment and never be sent back to Vietnam against their will.

He has referred to those people who have a passport in their back pockets while praising the coming jurisdiction of the People's Republic of China as the "Yacht People," which was widely considered by Hong Kong people to be an accurate definition.

A mix of his pertinent statements follow:

"It is said that Hong Kong should be part of China because geographically it is where it belongs—just look at a map. But ten years ago, if it was said that West Berlin should be part of East Germany because geographically that is where it belongs—just look at a map—what would the whole free world have done? And yet there is no response by some in the world about Hong Kong's turnover to China. No response; no argument.

"We will see Hong Kong be part of China. Hong Kong's six million citizens cherish our civil liberties and freedoms, principally because this territory is made up of several generations of refugees from China's political crackdowns, and we are acutely aware that these freedoms do not exist just a few short miles away, across the Chinese border.

"For Hong Kong, the most important part of the (new) international treaty was the promise that we, the people of Hong Kong, would have a fully elected legislature and would be allowed to govern ourselves with autonomy in all matters except for defense and foreign affairs, the people of Hong Kong increasingly find the long arm of China reaching into our daily lives: the bullying of politicians."

(Martin Lee and Szeto Wah had been labeled subversives by Beijing.)

"Hong Kong's Bill of Rights will have to be abolished after the 30th of June 1997, Chinese authorities announcing that our legislature and the two lower tiers of elected bodies will be axed when Beijing takes over in 1997. Democratic reform will be under attack, and as China's economic might and clout grow, so does its interest in absolute control over Hong Kong.

"Hong Kong's business community has been brought to heel with threats to remove Chinese trade, and companies and individuals supporting democratic reform have been targeted for retribution. These efforts are directed at crippling the powers and autonomy of Hong Kong's people during the transition period so there will be total control after 1997.

"Our great concern is that while Britain and China will continue to pay lip service to the Joint Declaration's promise of autonomy and 'one country, two systems'— at least until the takeover—in practice, Beijing wants strict control over Hong Kong well before 1997.

"It is clear to the people of Hong Kong that China is laying the groundwork for a very different Hong Kong after 1997.

"What will happen on July 1, 1997? It is almost impossible to tell what will happen. Frankly, I do not think that the Chinese even themselves know what they will do to Hong Kong on the 1st of July 1997. My guess is that nothing much will happen for the simple reason that the world will be here. Hong Kong will be crowded with reporters. One thing they will do is abolish the Legislative Council or replace it with a completely new one, replacing us with new faces or keep its faces and remove its authority. But I believe that nothing ghastly will happen that day. But slowly, maybe in a few months, things will happen. And so, it is important that the whole world watches what happens here. We must keep ourselves separate. Otherwise, we will have their corruption and their rule of man as opposed to the rule of law. We must keep ourselves separate, and that is what I intend to do.

"We want Hong Kong to be separate. We want Hong Kong to succeed in 1997, and even if we disagree on practically everything else, we must make sure that Hong Kong will be allowed to run its own affairs with minimal interventions. The theory is that there should be no intervention at all under the terms of the Joint Declaration. So before the First of July, 1997, we must show the Hong Kong people that democracy works. What I do not want to see happen in the coming months is my party fighting with the (British) Government on every single piece of the Hong Kong system. It will then be the verdict that the electoral reforms that resulted in this legislature are a failure; that democracy does not work for Hong Kong, and that is the last thing that we wish to see happen. If we can put our back together and show the people of Hong Kong that we can cooperate with our own government; that democracy works for Hong Kong and that it is good for Hong Kong, then come what may on the First of July 1997—they might demolish us, replace us, they could throw us into jail—the Hong Kong people have seen democracy at work, they loved it, and they would want to see it back in Hong Kong.

"As for the interest you have shown for my own fate, what would be the point of locking me up? I will now kowtow to them. But it's not impossible for them to lock me up on trumped-up charges. Some local business leaders tell me, 'The moment they lock you up, I start packing, because there's going to be little time between when they arrest you and when they come for me!'

"Those from abroad often ask why we do not fight for straight independence, a sovereignty of our own? A Canadian and I had a discussion here some time back and he asked me that. I said, 'Supposing we do want independence. Would your government support us?'

"He shook his head.

"I asked, 'Do you think the U.S. Government would support us?'

"He shook his head.

"'Can you think of any government that would support us?'

"He shook his head.

"'Would the U.N. support us?'

"He shook his head.

"And so we ask, instead, for the possible. President Bush signed the U.S.-Hong Kong Policy Act. The Act accepts that on the 1st of July 1997, Hong Kong will be turned to China, but that Hong Kong will be master over itself. So this act requires all U.S. Government Departments to treat Hong Kong as a separate entity from China after 1997. And so we ask to remind the Congress of that act. Because of that act, the State Department should look at Hong Kong separately.

"Now, in my last two visits to you in the States, I had high-level discussions with officials of the State Department, and I told them some of my interests and I was told on a number of occasions, 'I am sorry, Mr. Lee, there isn't much we can do. This is a very bad time for this. There is too much on the China plate.'

"And I said to these people, friends of mine, 'Look, if you guys have been doing a good job, there will always be a lot on the China plate. If you are pushing for this and you are pushing for that then, of course, there will always be too much on the China plate. But what is there on the Hong Kong plate? Nothing.' I said that on my last visit because I was not asking for a meeting with President Clinton, I was told he could not do it. That was the time you were involved with North Korea about the nuclear problems and so on. And you needed China's help with that one. And they said, 'We cannot do anything to aggravate the situation and ignore the Chinese help by giving you a meeting with the President or even the Vice President.'

"So I said, 'If there is a separate Hong Kong plate, why should there be a problem?' The little red book of the thoughts of Chairman Mao contains two sentences worth repeating, 'When the enemy advances, I retreat. When the enemy retreats, I advance.' Do you get the message?

"We know that so long as China's Communist leadership remains willing to sacrifice freedom on the altar of 'national stability,' the world may yet commemorate another tragedy—that the Hong Kong that once was is no more.

SZETO WAH was one of the two most prominent Hong Kong Legislators of the time. He was originally a prominent teacher and was one of the most distinguished Members of the Legislative Council of Hong Kong from 1985 through 2004. He was also Chairman of the Hong Kong Alliance in Support of a Patriotic Democratic Movement in China. Szeto Wah passed away in 2011 and is deeply missed.

The most unusual characteristic ever found in a politician is humility, and that fact is so unchallenged that it would never make print here if it weren't for Szeto Wah. When asked for a resume, he handwrote one—and it consisted of his education and teaching credential with little else. Unlike most Hong Kong people of his age at the time, he was born and educated and taught in Hong Kong and, other than brief close-by visits, has lived in Hong Kong throughout all those years.

His life was immersed in Hong Kong.

He had no foreign passport and did not want one. Beyond being a member of the Democratic Party (no relation to the party of the same name in the United States), he was easily re-elected to the Legislative Council. Along with Martin Lee, he was kicked out of the Basic Law Drafting Committee (BLDC) by Beijing. Although it is a tremendous medal of honor to have been kicked out, no mention is made of it from him as no mention was ever made of Szeto Wah by Szeto Wah.

The following are some of his remarks:

"Hong Kong needs to resist the forces that will demand it go backwards. Hong Kong must not retreat. And if Hong Kong can resist stepping back then it will be good for progress in China. When we talk about progress in

China, we are talking about both political and economic progress as one depends on the other, but the most important is political. Economic development will ultimately be determined by political progress.

"If Hong Kong does regress and retreat, this is what we might see for Hong Kong after 1997:

"The first thing Beijing will do is control, weaken, and ultimately eliminate the democratic forces here. They will re-draw the legislative districts, create large electoral districts with multiple seats, or they possibly will adapt proportional representation with multiple seats and single votes. I believe that the former is more likely: larger electoral seats and single votes. They will eliminate the nine new functional constituencies, returning back to only 21 constituencies. This will enable the pro-China factions to win easy victories. The ten-member Electoral Committee will also be revised according to the peculiar color of China's so-called democratic procedure. In this way, the strength of the democratic forces will, at most, be 15 to 20 seats. In addition, because the vast majority of the Executive Council is appointed and the Advisory Council is appointed, the pro-China party will also become the majority, the mainstream.

"The second thing China will do in Hong Kong is oppress the media; freedom of the press. They will use the purchase of newspapers, and they will put pressure on the owners of the newspapers who are in business on the mainland. They will buy senior administrators within the newspapers. They will control advertising. They will also threaten and frighten reporters, just as it is in the case of the Hong Kong reporter now who is imprisoned in China. The separation of powers into the legislative, judicial, and executive—and the fourth estate, the press—will be oppressed with restrictions becoming ever more severe.

"The third thing is bribery and corruption. What we see in China at the present time regarding money and power is unhealthy, and Hong Kong cannot avoid being infected with this after '97. Because if Hong Kong does not enjoy a high degree of democracy and self-rule, Hong Kong will not have and cannot have a strong ability to resist this bribery and corruption.

"The fourth thing is that the judiciary will find it increasingly difficult to maintain its independence and just character. The traditional attitude of the Chinese Communist Party is that the judiciary is a tool of one class against another. The recently passed decision regarding the Court of Final Appeal signals that the Communist Party will not hesitate to clearly and wantonly violate the Sino-British Agreement and the Basic Law. In the beginning, we will see certain political incidents happen: Problems will occur in the area of human rights. In the end, because of the intercourse and connection between money and power, even the economic conditions will not be able to avoid deterioration.

"The fifth thing that will happen is that every kind of human right and freedom will gradually be controlled. There will remain a small handful of pro-democracy people along with all kinds of people in small enterprises, medium-sized and large, people in the professions, even people in the pro-China party that will have a tough time of it.

"I hope that all of those that care about the future of Hong Kong will join together in trying to stop Hong Kong's regression, Hong Kong's retreat. If Hong Kong is able to maintain its current status and not retreat and not regress, then not only in economic, but in political terms, it will constitute a direct influence on mainland China. This is the role Hong Kong must have.

"Some people ask me, 'Can Hong Kong influence the mainland?' I say that the tail cannot wag the dog, but if the tail wags, it will have a healthy effect on the dog. Further, if you give a poison injection to the dog, the dog will die. If the dog dies, then the tail dies too."

"As individuals, I would ask you to encourage your U.S. media to establish news bureaus here. If, in the future, Hong Kong's local media is oppressed, censored, then the foreign bureaus can get out the news of what's happening here. Without the media, no one hears the sound of crying.

"I believe the U.S. can do more on the human rights front. For example, because of the U.S. attitude, Harry Wu was ultimately released. Right now, there are so many other political prisoners who do not receive that attention.

"Third is the Presidential Election of next year. Please put pressure on Presidential candidates regarding Hong Kong.

"Ultimately, progress in China will principally result from China itself, but pressure from the outside world cannot avoid being helpful.

"I am not calling for the United States to interfere in Hong Kong—but disinterest is a form of interference."

9

HOW HONG KONG
BECAME A BEACON
OF LIBERTY

Forgetting its romance and forgetting its visual spectacle, both of which are difficult to forget— the city worked and continues to work independently in freedom because of three elements.

The major element being the people. The inhabitants of Hong Kong prove on a daily basis that no one knows better what to do with liberty than those who have lived under an absence of liberty, and most of the builders of this city have known such an absence since they used to live across the border. Their constructions, their creations, their selling, their buying, their trading, their going from one place to another within Hong Kong are journeys that have no daily or nightly horizons of starting and stopping. The only deadline they have known since living in Hong Kong is 1997.

The second element was the British government. It did very little, which is exactly what any good government should do. Its regulations were very few and not the stifling of creativity and talent, and with almost a relaxed form of anarchy, yet there is little crime on the streets and a general feeling of safety no matter the hour. God-given civil liberties were not threatened. Throughout most of its history, its workers kept the fruits of their labor with only a flat rate tax of 15% (with some slight progressivity below 15% but not enough to talk about, and often not bothered with by the government or taxpayers) and only about two-fifths of the population paid any taxes at all, while tax evasion remained minimal. There has been a flat rate corporate tax of 16.5%, cut from 17.5%—no taxes on dividends and no sales taxes on most merchandise. There was no minimum wage law, yet Hong Kong has had, for decades, one of the highest average incomes in the world (surpassing Great Britain), while across the border in China, the average year's wages were generally outrageously low. And through most of those decades, the Hong Kong Government's annual report showed no deficit but, rather, a surplus. Welfare budgets remained low and limited to a fixed percentage of public spending that going up or down was dependent on the local economy. According to the World Health Organization, Hong Kong maintained the highest life expectancy in the world (Males = 75.1, Females = 81.4). The judicial system, with its established rule of law, had worked separate and apart from the executive and legislative arms of government; based on common law, but for too long, the executive and legislative branches have, in fact, not been separate. There had been an unelected legislature, which changed to a largely but not completely democratically elected legislature, and there had been a Chief Executive; the Governor in pre-handover days sent by London and had all real authority. The British were only .003 of the population of Hong Kong, but they governed little and well.

The third element of its sustained democracy can best be described as the Yixing Teapot: The old Chinese story is told that an old woman wanted to sell her teapot in the marketplace of Yixing. A foreign traveler came by and, at her invitation, he drank tea she poured from the teapot. It was the best tea he had ever tasted, and he offered to buy the teapot from her for a sum she never expected to be offered. While he went away to get the cash to pay her, she became conscious of the used appearance of the teapot, and because he offered her so much money for it, she scrubbed the teapot inside and out, not realizing that by removing the dross accumulated from years and years of tea leaves used in the pot, that she was removing what made every cup of tea as wonderful as it was. She, in fact, destroyed the very reason he wanted it.

Even a member of the Politburo of the People's Republic of China, Li Ruihuan, told the familiar story of the Yixing Teapot to the Chinese People's Political Consultative Conference in 1995. He did not make any specific parallel, but it was apparent to some that he was saying Hong Kong is today's Yixing Teapot and cannot be fooled with carelessly, or it will be destroyed.

Mainly, those three elements—the people and a benign government and the Yixing Teapot factor—have strongly made Hong Kong what it became and should remain: Hong Kong.

10

THE TIANANMEN
SQUARE MASSACRE

On the 15th of April 1989, twelve and one-half years after the death of Mao Tse-tung, the former Communist Party General Secretary Hu Yaobang died. Although lesser known worldwide than Mao Tse-tung who had been the Founder, the Chairman, and among other things, the President of the People's Republic of China, the death of Hu Yaobang had more of an impact on the next decade in China than the impact of the earlier death of Mao Tse-tung.

In life, Hu Yaobang had very little effect on events, although he strived to change the government. Little more than two years before Hu Yaobang died, he had issued a statement condemning the late Mao Tse-tung's Cultural Revolution. If that wasn't enough, even more courageously, Hu Yaobang talked in detail about the many then-current problems of China's rejection of democracy and human rights.

He was fired. Those statements of Hu were interpreted (correctly) as meaning that Deng Xiaoping, who had already replaced Mao's position of leadership, was guilty of creating or maintaining those problems. Deng Xiaoping explained his firing of Hu by saying that Hu failed to defend the People's Republic against the "sugar-coated bullets of the bourgeoisie." Deng also announced that Hu had "resigned" his position as Communist Party General Secretary after confessing to have "made mistakes on major issues of political principles."

Hu, who was also a member of the Politburo, stayed there and continued talking about the need for ending government corruption and nepotism. He advocated that the people be given their rights as prescribed in the People's Constitution. (As mentioned earlier, Article 35 of that Constitution stated that "Citizens of the People's Republic of China enjoy freedom of speech, of the press, of assembly, of association, of procession, and of demonstration.") At an early April 1989 meeting of the Politburo, while his colleagues taunted Hu's repeated criticisms of the government, Hu declared, "We have failed the people and the nation!" As soon as he got the words out, he collapsed in a heap and was carried out to a hospital. Within a week, he was dead.

The news of Hu's death traveled quickly in China by way of what was called "Small Lane News," which was the traveling whisper and the greatest communication device of China at the time. This method of communication was so effective that by the time Hu's death was publicly announced on the next day, it was already well known among the population of Beijing.

Particularly saddened by Hu's death were students of Beijing University who felt guilty for not speaking up for him when he was alive. They had regarded him as their champion, but he had suffered severely for such championship. The students went to Tiananmen Square on April 17 holding posters requesting that the government reappraise Hu's life, stating that he was a hero, not a villain. Posters read: "When You Were Deprived of Your Post, Why Didn't We Stand Up?" "We Feel Remorseful. Our Conscience Bleeds." "Those Who Should Die Still Live. Those Who Should Live Have Died." "Deng is Still Healthy at the Age of 84. Hu, who was only 73, has Died First." By day's end, some 500 students were in the square. These were the greatest acts of daring in China since students had hung posters on Democracy Wall a decade earlier. At this time, some of those students were still imprisoned for the posting of those messages ten years earlier.

Day by day, the demonstrations in Tiananmen Square enlarged. On the 18th of April, the 500 grew to 2000; the next day to 10,000 and that night to 40,000. Two days later, there were 100,000 in Tiananmen Square. Hu was no longer the major subject of their placards and slogans as the major itemized subjects became an end to government corruption, the advocacy of an independent judiciary, a free press, freedom of expression, and the right to choose their own jobs and careers. There were cries of "Deng Xiaoping and [Prime Minister] Li Peng: Hear Our Grievances!"

By the beginning of May, the students from Beijing University had been joined by students from thirty of Beijing's colleges and universities, and young people added to the crowd who came daringly from other provinces of China and even from the more distant British Crown Colony of Hong Kong. There appeared to be some safety in numbers, even more safety with President Mikhail Gorbachev of the Soviet Union scheduled to arrive in Beijing and to become the first Soviet leader to visit China in thirty years, and to be accompanied by one thousand journalists from all over the world with most of those journalists with the ability and ambition to witness events taking place in Beijing.

President Gorbachev was not taken to Tiananmen Square. Had he been taken there, he would have seen the biggest self-imposed crowd of all: one million Chinese in a demonstration for freedom.

That great city square, known for holding vast emptiness, had little emptiness left. To the great displeasure of Deng Xiaoping, Li Peng, and Mikhail Gorbachev, even the historical announcement of normalization of relations between the Soviet Union and the People's Republic of China took a backseat to the world's interest in the crowds of Tiananmen Square. The meetings and statements of the leaders became a sideshow to the story that was taking place in that square.

Gorbachev called the demonstrators "hot-heads." He went home and on his way back to Moscow, he lashed out at the government of the People's Republic of China for not containing those demonstrators.

Now, in a small courtyard of Beijing's Central Academy of Arts, twenty art students were secretly working with plaster and Styrofoam over a wooden frame to create a giant 33-foot statue called The Goddess of Democracy. The statue was being made in three parts with plans of having her sections wheeled to Tiananmen Square on three tricycle carts. Her right arm was extended upward, holding a torch. Her left hand was also extended in grasp of the lower part of the torch. She looked very much like a relation to New York's Statue of Liberty.

With Gorbachev back in Moscow, Deng Xiaoping met with the man whom he had previously selected to replace Hu Yaobang as Communist Party General Secretary: Zhao Ziyang. Deng was displeased to hear that Zhao had told Gorbachev that "political reform and economic reform should be synchronized. It won't do to lag behind in political reform." This was not what Deng wanted his new Communist Party General Secretary to say either publicly or privately. Deng was reported to have warned Zhao, "I have three million troops behind me!"

Zhao is said to have answered, "I have all the people of China behind me."

"You have nothing," was Deng's reported reply. There was little question that Zhao, like Hu before him, would not have a long tenure as Communist Party General Secretary.

During the dawn of the 19th of May, Zhao went to Tiananmen Square to express his sympathy with the protestors, particularly some 3,000 hunger-strikers with whom he sat and talked. With tears, he said to the demonstrators, "I came too late; too late. We deserve your criticism, but we are not here to ask your forgiveness." He asked them to end the hunger strike, and he signed his name on student's clothing.

On Saturday, the 20th of May, Prime Minister Li Peng went on television to decree martial law in Beijing. The demonstrators were ordered to leave Tiananmen Square or face twenty years imprisonment. The reaction of the demonstrators was to change their chants and posters to "Li Peng, Resign!" "Down with Li Peng!"

Before the day was done, the government announced that units of the People's Liberation Army would enter Beijing to restore order. After the directive was given, the Square's crowd became larger.

On the outskirts of the city, residents assembled on the main roads that could be used by the army so as to block them if the army was to attempt to enter. But they entered anyway, and when vehicles filled with soldiers came into the Square, those who stopped the troops gave them steamed buns, candies, and cigarettes. They read newspapers to them and told them to "love the people." There were embraces between the crowds of people and the troops. Many wept. The troops turned back.

Now the students in the Square were joined by people of all ages and from many walks of life.

The news from Tiananmen Square in Beijing created an epidemic of joining the protest, with thirty-four other cities in China expressing their solidarity with the students in Beijing and voicing that they were joining them in demonstration with the advocacy of democracy.

Threats continued to be given by the government through radio and television messages. Throughout the week, employers were told to tell their employees that if they missed any work they would lose their jobs. Two hundred thousand troops were now surrounding Beijing. Those in the square were being worn out, and for the first time since the protest began, demonstrators were leaving Tiananmen Square, just tired of it.

But something happened in the very late hours of the 29th of May. Students from Beijing's Central Academy of Arts wheeled in the three sections of the statue they had been building and assembling: The Goddess of Democracy. At first, it was difficult to make out what those huge packages were. As the statue was erected, first the base, then the robe-encased legs, then the top section of chest, head, arms, and hands holding the torch, the square became crowded again. Although it seemed illogical, as the crowd became larger, it became progressively quieter. In a short time the crowd was totally silent.

By the early hours of the 30th of May, the Goddess of Democracy stood without its surrounding wooden scaffolds. Then there was noise: there was cheering, and what was despair became a celebration and a revitalization. Throughout the day, the crowds kept increasing to see the statue that faced north toward the portrait of Mao Tse-tung.

The government was enraged at the statue and threatened the demonstrators that they either tear the statue down or face unspecified and severe punishments. The demonstrators didn't touch her except to lay flowers at her base, and students from Hong Kong surrounded the statue with blue and white pup tents and brilliant flags from colleges and universities.

A procession of tanks began advancing on East Chang'an Avenue toward the Square. (The rumbling procession looked and sounded like Unter den Linden in East Berlin in 1953 and Parizska Street in Prague in 1968 and TuDo Street in Saigon in 1975. It was the most imposing and ominous signal since the students came to Tiananmen Square in April.)

THEN CAME WANG WEILIN

East Chang'an Avenue had been cleared of auto and pedestrian traffic other than those who were in the area before barricades had been erected. The tanks, for which the avenue was cleared, were met by the most unlikely obstacle: one man, a slender young student in a white shirt, dark slacks, holding onto a small duffle bag of sorts and a jacket, obviously not having prepared himself for this moment. With his right hand he signaled for the tanks to halt. If they didn't, their path indicated they would run him over. They didn't.

Instead, the tanks stopped.

Then the drivers of the tank started again but tried to maneuver around him.

The slender man moved into their path regardless of their maneuver.

"He's crazy!" someone said softly.

"He's a Saint!" someone else said. "There's an aura about him. The tanks will stop."

The tanks stopped.

Then the drivers of the tank started again but tried to maneuver around him again.

The slender man moved into their path no matter their maneuver. He then climbed on the lead tank, and others on the sidewalks that were fearful of his fate ran to him and grabbed him and took him from the street.

"I think I know him," someone said. "He's so far away, but I think I know who he is."

"Do you know his name?"

"Yes. I'll spell it. W-A-N-G, W-E-I-L-I-N."

"Wang Weilin?"

"Yes. But I think it's pronounced Patrick Henry."

Unknown to the government, a photographer on a balcony of the Beijing hotel overlooking East Chang'an

Avenue had videotaped the young man as he faced the tanks. The young man's back was to the camera, the procession of tanks facing him. Prints of that image went around the world. The young man's strength of will remained beyond measurement. Many of those who took part in the liberation of their countries from the Soviet Union later that year referred to the inspiration and courage that the young man facing those tanks in China had given them.

THE ENLARGING MASSACRE

The Government of the People's Republic of China prohibited coverage of any demonstrations in Beijing, banning photographs, videotapes, and press coverage of any army troops acting in the enforcement of martial law. Then the army took up ten positions around Beijing, surrounding the city with troops. The news went all over the world despite the banning of press coverage.

In the pre-dawn hours of the 3rd of June, on East Chang'an Avenue toward Tiananmen Square came five thousand troops marching five abreast. There was another equal amount of troops coming down West Chang'an Avenue toward Tiananmen Square and a third amount of troops marching up Qianmen Street, the three masses forming a "T" converging on the square. Citizens of Beijing, along with some demonstrators from the square, rushed to the center of the "T" to stop them, forming a human obstacle before the soldiers could enter the square. From all directions, the marching of the soldiers stopped as they listened to the people, talked with them, and some soldiers embraced the people. There was little appetite among those troops to go into the square and put down the demonstration.

Then one soldier-filled jeep went right into the human barricade with total abandon. Three people were knocked down by the speeding jeep. They were killed. Other soldiers seemed as shocked and saddened as the civilians. It showed there was no consistency of motivation, and it was so senseless that they decided not to advance further on the Square.

The "Small Lane News" reaching the square was that Deng Xiaoping directed that the People's Liberation Army "must recover the Square at any cost."

The authenticity of his reported order was not confirmed, but throughout the day, some demonstrators were beaten, and some soldiers were hurt as well, and it was a standoff. More than the independent acts of fighting, there was a massive tension in the air that was undeniable. That tension was felt even by the least sensitive. It was like a silent countdown to catastrophe, and no one seemed to know when the countdown would be reached.

THEN CAME HELL

After sunset of 3rd of June, radio and television announced, "Do not come into the streets. Do not go to Tiananmen Square. Stay at home to safeguard your life."

On West Chang'an Avenue, a woman was kicked by five policemen until she fell. Then, as one held her hair, she was beaten with truncheons. A few feet from her, a man was beaten for over one minute. The police went away as the woman lay there unmoving and the man staggered with blood coming from gashes in his face and chest.

Before midnight, troops arrived in the city in greater mass than before, and this time, they were not as young and confused as the ones who were marching there during the day. There were not soldiers of the 38th Army who were young residents of Beijing, but professionals from the 27th Army from outside Beijing, arriving in armored vehicles that would not stop for those shouting at them. They fired their assault rifles into the crowds as they advanced forward and finally into the northern area of Tiananmen Square.

The citizens outside the square threw fire-bombs at them. One of the military's vehicles caught on fire, and the crowd killed a soldier. Other citizens grabbed crowbars and bricks and rocks and bottles and anything else that could be used as a weapon, as they heard that 350,000 soldiers were just outside Beijing from the 16th, 17th, 28th, 65th, and 69th Armies.

Outside Tiananmen Square, soldiers were beating all those who stood in their paths. Crowds started throwing bricks and rocks and bottles at them, and the soldiers fired back with AK-47s. People who lived in apartment buildings on Chang'an Avenue had to lie on the floor since bullets from AK-47s were firing in all directions. At the Minzu Hotel, a soldier killed a civilian in the lobby while other soldiers went to the occupant's balconies and shot down those in the street.

Casualties were lying on one street after another, many in pools of blood, their insides on the streets.

THE RADIO BROADCAST OF RADIO BEIJING

The Voice of America radio station had long been jammed, and that night the BBC was jammed as well. That left Radio Beijing to be singularly audible. This meant that the listeners to the English language service of Radio Beijing were to hear the most surprising commentary of its time and place:

"This is Radio Beijing. Please remember the 3rd of June 1989. The most tragic event happened in the Chinese capital, Beijing. Thousands of people, most of them innocent civilians, were killed by fully armed soldiers when they forced their way into the city. Among the killed are our colleagues at Radio Beijing. The soldiers were riding on armored vehicles and used machine guns against thousands of local residents and students who tried to block their way. When the army convoys made a breakthrough, soldiers continued to spray their bullets indiscriminately at crowds in the street. Eyewitnesses say some armored vehicles even crushed foot soldiers who hesitated in front of the resisting civilians. Radio Beijing English Department deeply mourns those who died in the tragic incident and appeals to all its listeners to join our protest for the gross violation of human rights and the most barbarous suppression of the people. Because of this abnormal situation here in Beijing, there is no other news we could bring you. We sincerely ask for your understanding and thank you for joining us at this most tragic moment."

The unidentified voice was never heard on radio again, or perhaps from anywhere again.

Then, as though a scene from one movie was spliced into a film of another, Prime Minister Li Peng gave a radio and state television speech on, of all things, the environment. It had nothing to do with the news coming from Tiananmen Square. Instead, Li Peng was talking about clean air and pollution as though he was a member of Greenpeace with his image painted by Salvador Dali.

BACK TO WHAT HAD BECOME THE NORMAL INSANITY IN BEIJING

Midnight passed, and the massacre of the surrounding streets began and was soon to become known as the massacre of Tiananmen Square, which was now in a fury as troops moved into the Square from all directions.

Tanks and other Armored Personnel Carriers ran over tents in Tiananmen Square although it was known that students were in the tents. The soldiers poured gasoline over the demolished tents and over the flattened bodies, and then put flames to the poured gasoline.

At least thirty-three carts, with each carrying three dead bodies, were wheeled away shortly after the Army opened fire.

Doctors attempting to heal the wounded were killed. Hospitals were instructed by the government not to reveal how many had been brought to their doors or how many the hospitals listed as dead. The bodies were not allowed to be given to their families.

Some students in the Square linked their arms together

to form a wall in front of advancing soldiers. The soldiers stopped to kneel and spray the crows with live bullets. The line of students fell to the ground from left to right.

Bodies were everywhere, and on the pavement, there were long patterns of blood from where the bodies had been dragged away.

Sunrise was not sunrise. The sun was invisible behind the gray and the smoke. Bodies were strewn throughout the Square. As bodies were picked up by those daring enough to remain in the Square, many of the rescuers were shot by soldiers and became motionless bodies themselves.

Beijing hospitals had quickly verified 700 deaths in the massacre. Amnesty International estimated that the number was a minimum of 1,000. The Red Cross gave the figure of 2,600 until the Red Cross was ordered by the government of the People's Republic of China to deny that report. Other estimates were as high as 10,000. Precise figures were unknown since so many of the corpses were burned on the spot, while other bodies were put on helicopters to be taken to locations unknown, and the living were warned to remain silent.

It was just a little past five o'clock of that gray morning when one tank headed toward the Goddess of Democracy and smashed her to the ground.

The following day, U.S. President Bush announced immediate sanctions against China with a suspension of military equipment, a suspension of government-to-government trade, and he said Chinese students in the United

States could apply to extend their visas.

Within ten days after the Tiananmen Square Massacre, the Government of the People's Republic of China arrested over a thousand of those still living who they believed were dissenters who had been in the Square.

It was not confirmed, but it was said through the "Small Lane News" that the young man who had stood up to the tanks was Wang Weilin, and he had been executed on June 17th. Although it was confirmed by others, another said he had heard it was the 18th.

There were quick "trials" and executions of demonstrators, with one captured demonstrator after another paraded on television, all with bowed heads and hands cuffed behind backs appearing before a "court." They were students that had been photographed, interviewed, and praised throughout the world as heroes before the massacre began. No more. Now they would be executed.

A dozen days after the massacre, on the 16th of June, Deng Xiaoping said that once he stabilized the political situation and the economy was improving, foreigners would be back knocking on his door. (He was unrealistically pessimistic. Some foreigners were back before the political situation had been stabilized and before the economy was higher again.)

There were house-to-house searches in Beijing with government authorities asking every household where its occupants were and what they were doing in April, May, and June. The government urged residents to tell what they knew about others during that period and that it was a patriotic duty to turn in members of their own families. Telephone hotlines were instituted for informers who wanted to be anonymous. Every workplace was required to have new committees established that would investigate everyone else at work, while second committees were established to investigate the primary committees.

On the 19th of June, the Communist Party Central Committee issued a directive called "Document Number Three," stating that the number of people imprisoned and executed would no longer be published. It also stated a small amount of imprisoned would be relieved so as to serve as examples. It appeared that they were attempting to tell the world that all was well, while still causing fear in their own citizens.

On the 20th of June, Zhao Ziyan, who had sympathized with the students, was purged from his job as General Secretary of the Communist Party and placed under house arrest. He was replaced with a loyalist, the party chief of Shanghai, Jiang Zemin. (In 1992, Jiang Zemin would be named President as well as General Secretary.)

On the same day, the 20th of June 1989, President George H.W. Bush established a ban on all high-level diplomatic talks between U.S. officials and officials of the People's Republic of China.

Near the beginning of July (the precise date was not announced publicly but it was only weeks at most after the 20th of June), National Security Advisor, Brent Scowcroft, and Deputy Secretary of State, Larry Eagleburger, flew to Beijing for high-level meetings. It was unofficially revealed on the 17th of December and had been held under wraps for months that it occurred and that the visit had taken place to personally underscore the U.S. shock and concern over the crackdown. Then Brent Scowcroft and Larry Eagleburger went to Beijing again on the 9th and the 10th of December. The stated purpose of those two further visits was to tell Deng Xiaoping and Li Peng what happened at the Malta meetings between President Bush and Soviet President Gorbachev. Without knowing all the information on the visits, it is difficult to determine if the decision for the visits was right or wrong, but with great confidence and trust in President George H.W. Bush, his reasoning might well have included non-public facets that were better served in public invisibility and inaudibly. Naturally and repeatedly, most high-level meetings are no stranger to items of such validity.

THE SHADOW OF THE TIANANMEN SQUARE MASSACRE IN BEIJING LINGERS LARGE AND LONG IN HONG KONG

In Hong Kong's Victoria Park, police reported some one million people holding candles, with more than one-sixth of the entire population of the entire Hong Kong territory standing there in silence. At the center of the massive crowd was a giant replica of the Goddess of Democracy, taller than the original that had stood in Tiananmen Square.

Szeto Wah started at the base of the statue and spoke to the crowd through what seemed to be hundreds of loud-speakers. (He spoke in Cantonese.) Some of the organizers were passing out pieces of paper. "We have English," one of the organizers said, and he handed a piece of paper to those who nodded at him.

The paper that was passed out to the candleholders told that troops had mopped up Tiananmen Square by burning and removing bodies, and in the absence of more targets in the Square, the killing had expanded.

The bottom of the paper had a statement of US President Bush: "I deeply deplore the decision to use force against peaceful demonstrators and the consequent loss of life. We have been urging and continue to urge non-violence, restraint, and dialogue. Tragically, another course has been chosen. Again, I urge a return to non-violent means for dealing with the current situation."

Any remaining optimism among the Hong Kong people and their international supporters was smothered by the revelations told by those who became Tiananmen Square victims and lived, then disguised themselves and escaped capture in Beijing, by daring to take trains southward into Hong Kong while claiming all kinds of made-up stories told to Beijing uniformed observers as to why they were traveling from Beijing to Hong Kong.

After some safely got away with their impersonations of travelers supposedly making it into Hong Kong to buy watches and other gifts for friends, they headed for Hong Kong coffee shops and talked to patrons who would listen— including officials of the Hong Kong press to whom they told some of their first-hand experiences of being beside victims in the now world-known Massacre that the People's

Republic would refer to simply as the non-defined phrase, "the June 4th Incident."

Americans who coincidentally were in those Hong Kong coffee shops listened to the accounts of those patrons who had been in Tiananmen Square.

In contrast, the Chinese demonstrators in Tiananmen Square had been immersed in something far different than known in the United States. It was clear that Tiananmen Square was not the American-known Potomac Park with the smell of marijuana and crowded sleeping bags as strangers searched for physical pleasures, nor was it an arena for cowardice to be justified by slogans of false innocence. This was something different. The only similarities to those crowds in Washington D.C. were the smells of unchanged clothes and the noises and disorder, but all that had paled in minutes, and those particular young people who had been demonstrators in Tiananmen were welcome as they were: good because there was something that permeated these young people while reeking of an ageless and timeless importance. One held a small placard that confirmed that timelessness with the hand-printed words on that placard; "Let My People Go" in both Chinese and English.

In years ahead, if one member of a family or friend of the family was a dissenter in Tiananmen Square, the family or friend would be watched by a PRC government organization not previously known. This watch-list had no public forecast of when or if the observation would end—but the rumors were many.

11

TIANANMEN SQUARE
POSTSCRIPT

(This is a temporary advancement of the calendar but is significant to be placed here. This book will return to the preceding chronology after this postscript is recorded here, where it should be done regardless of format.)

On the 14th of October 2016, a man who was somewhere between 51 and 54 years old was released from a Beijing prison after having been arrested in 1989 when he was 27 years old. The imprisonment resulted in sadistic tortures that lasted through every day and every night.

His prison sentence was that lengthy and horribly spent because he was a protestor against the government of the People's Republic of China during the Tiananmen Square Massacre. That government spokesperson said he was the last person released who had been taken prisoner during what they called "the June 4th incident" in Tiananmen Square. Although his name is well known, his name will not be told here, nor will his details of imprisonment be told here. It is enough to say that he is a great man, imprisoned by evil humans for evil reasons. He should be remembered for his greatness and not for his being forced to undergo the unthinkable years of uncivilized inhumanity.

12

(AND THIS BOOK IS NOW BACK TO ITS NORMAL CHRONOLOGY)

HOW BRITAIN HAD ITS FIRST NAME OF "GREAT" RE-ESTABLISHED IN HONG KONG

With the Tiananmen Square Massacre considered to be history, on the 4th of April 1990, The Basic Law for Hong Kong was presented by the People's Republic of China for the years 1997-2047. In brief, it was and remains a terrible Mini-Constitution for the people of Hong Kong dealing with the takeover of the People's Republic of China.

Although that revelation of the new Basic Law for Hong Kong was one of many current bad breaks for Hong Kong people, there was one wonderful break ahead, but it took a few years to come to be on the 9th of July 1992. The break was that Christopher Francis Patten was named the new British Governor of Hong Kong.

This was not the usual small matter of the appointment of another Governor. In this case, he was the 28th Governor and not a small matter because his presence in that office made Hong Kong people use the word "Great" once again to consistently precede the word "Britain." That was because Governor Patten became the most outspoken, pro-liberty, independence-seeking Hong Kong Governor in the history of Hong Kong. That made him a Governor walking a tight-rope stretched between the people of Hong Kong, his home government in London, and the People's Republic of China.

But of course, as he knew (and this is not said lightly but with accuracy), he could not simply create and administer a new law that would relinquish any laws made by the leader of the People's Republic of China that loved to decree only oppressive things for Hong Kong people. In short, the PRC leader would never allow the lesser office of the Governor to rule that the people of Hong Kong make sure the leader of the PRC give up any bad news for them. They had learned from the history of Tibet that the worse the bad thing might be, the longer and more precisely it must be obeyed.

And so it was that when, in 1993, Governor Patten appointed Anson Chan as his Chief Secretary (who would then automatically be the Second in Command and Acting Governor in the Governor's absence), there was a quick PRC revival of the customary unlucky breaks for Hong Kong as the officials of the Government of the PRC were soon dealing only with her instead of Governor Patten. Those in the Government of the People's Republic of China did not want to speak at all with Governor Patten. It was clear that their duty to those who served the PRC's government was that Governor Christopher Francis Patten be determined to be of no service to that government. The only large body of those who were delighted with Governor Patten's ability to be Governor was the great majority of Hong Kong people.

His appointment and the PRC's reaction became a proven prologue of events to come when, on the 25th of February 1994, the PRC vowed to disband any and all elected bodies in Hong Kong as soon as the PRC would take control in 1997.

In June of 1995, the prologue for the rules of the 1997 takeover continued as an agreement was reached regarding the Court of Final Appeal, with Great Britain giving in to every demand of the PRC.

Then, in September of 1995, an election for the members of Hong Kong's Legislative Council (LEGCO) was held. It was the first fully elected Legislative Council in Hong Kong's history, and to the PRC's dismay, the election brought about the overwhelming victory of democracy advocates. There would still be no pouring of champagne in Hong Kong as the PRC said the electing of the Legislative Council made no difference, as they had already announced the Legislative Council would be dissolved on the 1st of June 1997. The fact that the normal elections placed the winners in office for four-year terms—that would under old circumstances take them to 1999 in the autonomous region of Hong Kong—was immaterial to the PRC. The PRC announced that the PRC-appointed Preparatory Committee would replace the elected Legislative Council with a provisional body until elections would be held under PRC-approved rules.

The local Bill of Rights Ordinance was a combination of the International Covenant on Economic, Social, and Cultural Rights known as the ICESCR. (If you don't care about this, don't worry about it. It doesn't make much difference. It's just added here for accuracy.) In view of the strong support of the International Bill of Rights throughout Hong Kong, the Bill of Rights Ordinance had already been enacted years back, making local law out of the international covenants observed in Hong Kong since 1976. And although the Sino-British Joint Declaration had similarly guaranteed that the provisions of the two covenants as applied to Hong Kong should remain in force after 1997, China backed out of that in November of 1995 and scheduled itself to go deeper and deeper in cutting the Bill of Rights as the years went on.

But Governor Patten was not discouraged by the continuing rules from the PRC once again: In October of 1995, he advocated that Great Britain give all those qualifying for

British passports in Hong Kong (3.3 million) "the right of abode" in Great Britain should they choose to live there. In November of 1995, the People's Republic of China announced its intention to weaken Hong Kong's Bill of Rights Ordinance.

In December of 1995, Wei Jingsheng, a democracy advocate in China, was sentenced to 14 years imprisonment (after having served 15 years previously for his pro-democracy activities.) A Hong Kong demonstration in support of Wei Jingsheng was filled with signs saying, "Today it's Mr. Wei (pronounced "Wee"). Tomorrow It's You and Me."

The People's Republic of China seemed to continue to be unable to understand that political and economic freedoms cannot be independent of one another and that they travel a path of broken promises for other "autonomous regions," including Tibet and Shanghai. And there were increasingly more than the seven million people of Hong Kong who built that magnificent city who wanted and continue to want that city—more than anything else—to live in liberty.

And there is the United States of America, whose role has been made and sometimes re-made by succeeding Presidents, as most often each U.S. President re-reads or should re-read the 1936 U.S. Supreme Court decision that grants foreign policy to be the business of the U.S. President and not the U.S. Congress (U.S. v. Curtiss Wright Export Corporation), who, in recent times, has often assumed they can make the foreign policy decisions.

One of the most unexpected events in the Pre-1997

chronology occurred in October 1995 with the statement of Governor Patten calling on his nation, Great Britain, to give the right of abode to all the 3.3 million Hong Kong residents who qualified for passports. Great Britain's Home Secretary Michael Howard quickly said it would not be done.

Governor Patten answered, "I don't think that three million Hong Kong citizens are suddenly going to arrive at Heathrow. Nobody seriously supposes that and, if they did, they certainly wouldn't be living on the welfare state." What he wanted was the concern of the Chinese Government so that they would be more sensitive in their treatment of Hong Kong, knowing the people there could leave if that be their choice. Governor Patten called it a "Passport Wagon."

John Carlisle of Great Britain's Parliament answered, "Britain should not become a dumping ground for every traveling Chinaman."

With all the scorn of so many of his countrymen, Governor Patten received at least the praise of many Hong Kong people represented by the highly respected democracy legislative leaders, Martin Lee Chu-ming and Szeto Wah, who exclaimed both surprise and pleasure at Governor Patten's advocacy. And there were new labels given to him from the People's Republic of China who, even more markedly, turned their back on him with the claim that he is "irrelevant."

On the 19th of December 1995, the PRC announced that during the transition period, "The last colonial governor cannot represent Britain."

To quell the anger in Hong Kong, particularly

uproarious after the Tiananmen Square Massacre of 1989, Great Britain's Parliament passed the British Nationality (Hong Kong) Act of 1990, giving an additional 50,000 heads of households the "right of abode" in Great Britain, which also included their dependents, for a total of approximately 225,000 Hong Kong people. The People's Republic of China quickly said they would not recognize those passports when they took over. The Chinese Foreign Ministry issued a statement saying, "This move of the British side contravenes the spirit and essence of the Chinese-British Joint Declaration and impairs China's sovereignty. It is unacceptable to the Chinese Government."

The response to take advantage of the new British policy was much less than expected, some of that due to China's response, some of it due to England not being a favored place to live if other places were available and, perhaps most of all, due to the incomprehensibility of its legal jargon, a difficult point system imposed, and a complex 30-page application, which some felt was designed to make the applicant give up.

Among those who assumed they wouldn't qualify, it was said that the British were being elitist through a policy of great selectivity, particularly qualifying the rich, and the British should give "right of abode" normal British passports to all 3.3 million in Hong Kong qualifying for a British passport (already holding the weathering British Dependent Territories Citizen passport.)

Some other governments had an opportunity in all

of this: A passport could be bought from Singapore for $500,000. Costa Rica's price became $34,000 if the person lived there for four months out of a year for five years, then became a citizen. Ireland offered a passport for $1.5 million being invested into an approved business enterprise that "created long-lasting employment for Irish citizens." A Fiji passport cost $30,000 plus an investment of $100,000 in Fiji-approved businesses. Tonga's cost was $25,000. The Caribbean British offered competitive prices for passports with different requirements of "registration fees" and investments. A newspaper advertisement in Hong Kong, and a mailed brochure, promised a nationality document in Conterra in the South Seas for only $5,000. Whoever placed the advertising and distributed the brochure made a fortune, and complaints poured in from those who sent their money and later found out Conterra did not exist.

Approximately ten percent of Hong Kong residents (approximately 600,000) had foreign passports, one way or another, and it wasn't over. An average of over 1,000 Hong Kong people had been leaving Hong Kong per week in the period right after the Tiananmen Square massacre. Ronald Skeldon of the University of Hong Kong's Geography Department was part of a group conducting emigration surveys and he arrived at the conclusion that 780,000 would leave by the time of the takeover in 1997. Michael DeGolyer, Director of the Hong Kong Transition Project at Hong Kong Baptist College, led another survey team and said the total would be more than one million.

Michael DeGoyler added, "That's a very conservative number based on what we know." He said there are 450,000 expatriates in Hong Kong, about 400,000 others with the "right of abode" somewhere else, and more than two million with a foreign-based close family member who could serve as a sponsor.

Even Dame Lydia Dunn, the Hong Kong icon who was born in Hong Kong and was the first Chinese person named to Britain's House of Lords, "[left] Hong Kong for family reasons."

(More than half the companies listed on Hong Kong's stock exchange now listed their legal domicile in Bermuda or the British West Indies. Bermuda, after all, is a British colony whose people had just voted overwhelmingly to retain that status rather than be independent from Great Britain, causing Prime Minister Swan, who was an independence-advocate, to resign.)

Canada and Australia were then the most popular new homes of Hong Kong individuals who left, particularly Vancouver, Canada, where there were "Widow Streets" harboring wives of Hong Kong businessmen while their husbands were still working in Hong Kong. Canada gave the right of Canadian residency to the families, and the right of refuge to any who might want to flee Hong Kong at a moment's notice.

If diplomacy is an art (and it is), Governor Patten was compatible with a Governor Michelangelo attempting to paint a 409 square mile Sistine Chapel Ceiling, but who had to use a palette with colors he inherited rather than mixed himself, and with his diverse over-seers watching every brush-stroke. Governor Patten said:

> "Chinese officials are always very sensitive about some-thing they call internationalization. But the fact of the matter is that this is a city which becomes part of China in 1997. It is also an international city, full of people from other parts of the world. It is one of the great cities of the globe, a great trading city, like New York or Venice or Amsterdam or London at their peaks of prosperity, and it could be, analysts say—I was reading one of those futurologists the other day who said that by the year 2010, 2020—Hong Kong, on present trends, would become the richest city in the world. Now it's not surprising, under these circumstances, that the world takes an interest in what happens here.
>
> "I think Chinese officials, in their hearts, know that. I think that's why one very distinguished Chinese leader recently said that the world would be looking at how China handles this precious teapot; how China manages to go on pouring very good tea out of this precious teapot.
>
> "I think that Chinese officials know, in their hearts, that the rest of the world is going to regard the way one country; two systems works after 1997; the way Beijing relates to Hong Kong as a sort of litmus test for how China is going to behave in the region and in the

world, as its greatness as a nation is manifested in the role that it plays on the international stage. So, speaking so, speaking for myself without in any way wishing to construct conspiracies or surround China in any unfair way, I very much hope that our friends around the world will continue to take an interest, will continue to visit, will continue to write, will continue to make programs, will continue to report, will continue to make their views felt, just as I'm sure Chinese people going to other places make their thoughts about them manifest as well.

"There are many guarantees for Hong Kong's civil liberties. There's the Basic Law, there's the International Covenants, there's the Joint Declaration. But the most important guarantee is people's commitment to those civil liberties. Example: reporting what's going on. Self-censorship, which journalists very often worry about, can only be dealt with by not allowing oneself to be censored. It's easier for me to say it, I concede straightaway, because I won't be here after 1997. But who knows: there may even be a little self-censorship today.

"Nobody thinks that between now and 1997 the Governor of Hong Kong is going to roar around the territory trampling on people's civil liberties. The reassurances that people look for have to be given by China and Chinese officials in deeds as well as words. And I very much hope that they will give reassurances in the next couple of years. It's in all our interests. This is a unique place. It's a very, very precious place. And all of us should want it to stay that way."

He will be known as the first Governor of Hong Kong to attempt to bring about a democratic framework for Hong Kong, since previously supported policies were often to nod at China who did not want documented democracy in that territory. The framework was coming too late, but it still took courage.

Almost as soon as Chris Patten arrived in Hong Kong back in 1992, he introduced bills to replace the appointment of local council members by the governor with elected numbers, to lower the voting age from 21 to 18, to increase the number of elected members of the Legislative Council, and to expand electoral participation for those seats in the Council that had been indirectly elected by professional constituencies. The proposals were modest in terms of democracy, but for Hong Kong, they were explosive. And the fact that he proposed important changes without seeking the approval of the People's Republic of China was something that had not been done since the 1997 framework was discussed between Thatcher and Deng.

Democracy advocates celebrated that they finally seemed to have an ally in Government House while the Government of the People's Republic of China was outraged at his "outlandish, audacious, and criminal behavior," while a minimum of Hong Kong placed itself on China's side, scared to death of the displeasure of that government.

Governor Patten hit back:

"This is one of the most sophisticated economic communities in the world, well-traveled, well educated, hugely successful economically.

"I, too, hope we will be able to make at least some progress in convincing Chinese leaders that this hugely precious community, representing as it does twenty-three percent of Chinese GNP, succeeds not just because of some capitalist equation but because its way of life helps to sustain its prosperity as well as its prosperity helping to sustain its way of life."

The Government of the People's Republic of China's voice was loud and clear. It announced that come the 1st of July 1997, they may well not honor contracts made with Hong Kong prior to the takeover, and they would abolish all three tiers of Hong Kong Government established before the 1st of July 1997.

It did not go unnoticed that Governor Patten was advocating policies that London did not invent, and in some cases, probably did not even endorse. Governor Patten was walking the highest wire of appointed political lives. There was no way some element wouldn't attempt to push him down, as those elements measured his every step: his own government in London, the democracy advocates of Hong Kong, the frightened non-political community of Hong

Kong, the People's Republic of China that would take over no matter what he might do, and his own conscience, which was on the side of the democracy advocates.

Beijing, never subtle with language (officially calling the United States during the Vietnam War days as "running dogs"), continually called Governor Patten "a criminal."

Following his conscience, Governor Patten continued to advocate democratic changes that challenged the People's Republic of China and, at times, challenged London. (London could always replace him—but they didn't. The People's Republic of China would obviously replace him, but there was still time.) In his quest of ensuring more confidence for the people of Hong Kong in their future, he advocated that the Court of Final Appeal, the highest court of the Hong Kong Judiciary (replacing the Privy Council of Great Britain as Hong Kong's highest court), should run as a "through train" starting prior to 1997 going right through the takeover date and into the future. He also publicly advocated that the Court of Final Appeal should have two overseas judges out of its five members, so that at least two would be knowledgeable and experienced in the common law. Further, he said that he wanted it established that Beijing would not have the ability to go above the decisions of the Court of Final Appeal other than in acts of state, and those acts of state would be defined by Great Britain's common law, already identified as those acts solely involving foreign affairs and defense pre-1997.

In June of 1995, it was decided. Chris Patten won

none of those things he advocated. But he defended the orders of Beijing. The Court of Final Appeal would not be established until after the takeover on the 1st of July 1997; there would only be, at most, one foreign judge rather than two; and Beijing would have jurisdiction over and above the Court of Final Appeal in acts of state "such as" foreign affairs and defense. The words "such as" permitted a wide scope of unknowns. "Such as" could mean anything the People's Republic of China would say it would mean—case to case. Unfortunately, those were the words that were used in Article 19 of The Basic Law, although the earlier Joint Declaration, upon which the Basic Law was supposed to be based, had read "the Hong Kong Special Administrative Region will enjoy a high degree of autonomy, except for-eign and defense affairs which are the responsibilities of the Central People's Government." (Page 11, Numeral 3[2]). Someone in Beijing made a quick change from the Joint Declaration to the Basic Law and carried it through to the decision of the Court of Final Appeal.

Governor Patten said of the Court of Final Appeal, "I think it was a good deal on both sides. Not every deal with China is a sellout or bad for Hong Kong."

The democracy advocates of Hong Kong were outraged at Governor Patten's defense of such a decision, calling it a "betrayal" after he publicly advocated exactly the opposite of what Beijing decided. There was a "no-confidence vote in Patten" held in the Legislative Council. He survived it 35 to 17, but not before powerful voices let it be known that he was no longer their champion. One of the two most respected voices in Hong Kong, the voice of legislator Martin Lee Chu-ming, said the Governor had kowtowed to the People's Republic of China and "it must be painfully obvious to all that this Court of Final Appeal agreement was wholly in Britain's' interests and Governor Patten has now abdicated all his principles and responsibilities to Hong Kong...It's a calculated condemnation of the Hong Kong people to the grimmest possible future...Hong Kong people will never be able to challenge the Beijing government... the capitulation (of the Governor on the Court of Final Appeal) opens the door to all political or sensitive cases being deemed 'acts of state' by the Beijing central government."

Governor Patten answered back that "there is a middle-ground between confrontation and kowtowing" and, "I spent three years being lambasted for being too aggressive, too assertive in standing up for Hong Kong...One deal with China and suddenly, Martin Lee and others are saying 'It's all over, the game is up.'"

On the 17th of September 1995, an election for four-year seats in the Legislative Council was held. For the first time in Hong Kong's history, due to Governor Patten's plan, all sixty members would be elected, with none appointed by the Governor. The electoral system was a combination of three tiers: 20 seats to be decided by geographical con-stituencies (by residents of districts), 30 seats to be decided by functional constituencies (by profession or craft), and 10 seats to be decided by election committee (by electors).

The results of the September 17 election were not what Beijing wanted—or expected—as Beijing had mounted a serious campaign for their candidates. By and large, democracy advocates enjoyed massive victories. Martin Lee Chuming proclaimed, "Hong Kong people voted with their hearts and minds for freedom and genuine democracy."

Gary Cheng Kai Nam of the pro-Beijing party, The Democratic Alliance for the Betterment of Hong Kong (who lost his election) said that the colony's six million people would "have to pay" for their choice.

Cheng Shousan, Deputy Director-General of the Hong Kong and Macau Affairs Office (a front for the People's Republic of China), said that future candidates for local offices in Hong Kong would have to be proven loyal to Beijing and that freedom in Hong Kong would not be unrestricted, but come with "some limits and bounds."

A Foreign Ministry spokesman for the People's Republic of China, Chen Jian, gave his government's view: "We don't think this election truly reflects the will of the Hong Kong people." Without any logic of basis, a spokesman for the Xinhua News Agency (which acts as the "Embassy" of the People's Republic of China in Hong Kong) said, "The results showed that hope for a smooth transition and love of the motherland and Hong Kong remain the main trend in Hong Kong."

Deng Xiaoping didn't make a statement, but the ailing "paramount leader" hadn't made a statement on anything in some time. In the absence of a fresh statement, *Ta Kung Pao,* the Beijing-run Hong Kong newspaper, dusted off a 1987 statement of Deng Xiaoping. *Ta Kung Pao* ran an article stating that Deng believed that popularly elected officials wouldn't be the best choice to administer Hong Kong, and instead, it should be run by "Hong Kong people who love Hong Kong and China."

Democracy advocates in the legislature reminded Beijing that they had just been elected for four-year terms. The reality, however, was not bright. Beijing immediately repeated that the Legislative Council would be dissolved on the 1st of July 1997, no matter that the winners were elected to four-year terms. Instead, they would serve only through the 30th of June 1997.

Governor Patten said:

> It seems to be an astonishing way of trying to win the hearts and minds in Hong Kong to say, at the moment when the people of Hong Kong are taking part in the most credible and democratic election in our history, that you are going to give the whole thing thumbs down.

In some respects, it was also a tough election for the Governor because, through the remainder of his term, he would be faced with a Legislative Council that would fight him on every measure that might be in any way concilia-tory to Beijing, but that at the same time might be ordered to be endorsed by London. But he was the one who reformed the electoral process so that he couldn't appoint members as Governors previously did. The reforms that were his own invention were now in effect through the rest of his administration, and he took pained pride in living with them.

Governor Patten said, "After this is over (July 1, 1997), I'm certain I'm going to have earned some time with a good book under a tree."

No one fought him on that one.

13

TWO SIDE-SHOWS AWAY
FROM CENTER STAGE

THE FIRST SIDE-SHOW: THE CHEP LAP KOK AIRPORT

One of the most unlikely controversies in the transition of Hong Kong from Great Britain to the People's Republic of China was the building of a new airport. The People's Republic of China was suspicious from the beginning that Great Britain was pulling a fast one by giving contracts to British builders, using up reserves, and leaving little or nothing for the People's Republic of China on the 1st of July 1997.

Governor Chris Patten argued back that the Chinese Government would "receive the biggest dowry since Cleopatra."

Chinese Premier Li Peng answered the Governor with, "The British Empire has taken far more wealth out of Hong Kong during its century-plus rule since 1840 than what it is leaving behind in its 'dowry' in 1997." (In 1991, Great Britain said the People's Republic of China would probably inherit at least $3.3 billion, but it then looked as though it would be more like $20 billion and scheduled to double by 1999 because of advancing land sales.)

What Li Peng didn't say was that the PRC was looking toward surplus funds inherited from Hong Kong to build Asia's biggest naval station on Stonecutters Island (now land-filled) off Kowloon. The airport debate was harsh between the two sides, although there was no debate that a new airport was needed.

The Hong Kong airport, Kai Tak, had been in operation since the 1920s for short hops, and since 1936 for flights between Hong Kong and Great Britain, and then it became a world-wide international airport, and then the third-busiest airport in the world. Hosting more than 24 million passengers a year, it was necessary to turn away over 330 flights a week. Kai Tak had only one runway for newer jets and that runway was partly in the middle of the harbor, still requiring airliners to approach it between high-rise buildings in the middle of the city.

Because of its long history, it seemed to be a tragedy that

Kai Tak would soon be gone, bulldozed out of existence and replaced with shopping centers and housing units, another part of the urban sprawl. (Even its name, Kai Tak, seemed filled with romance until it was learned that it didn't mean anything other than the builder's names: Mr. Kai and Mr. Tak. So maybe it's okay that by putting sentiment aside, it had to be bulldozed.)

After years of controversy over the new airport, with the controversy continuing while it started to be built, an agreement was reached between Great Britain and the PRC, with the PRC victorious in being able to accept or reject all pre-1997 decisions, including contracts on the airport, as well as financial guarantees by the British. And so, the new Chep Lap Kok Airport just west of Hong Kong on Lantau Island (or more accurately, most of it an extension of Lantau Island on reclaimed land) became scheduled for completion in April of 1998.

The construction was the largest construction project in the world (or at least was at the time); so large it could be seen from a satellite, and its cost of somewhere over $20 billion was around six times the cost of the then-new Denver Airport. Along with the airport was planned a new city, Tung Chung, with schools, hospitals, and shopping centers, and enough residences for 20,000 people to begin with, and eventually 200,000. It would take only 23 minutes to get from the new airport to Central on Hong Kong Island (21 miles) by rail via Tsing Vi and Kowloon, with a train leaving the airport every eight minutes. A helicopter service would provide guests of the Peninsula Hotel with a ride of only eight minutes. There was planned two suspension bridges with two decks, one for six lanes of automobile traffic and the lower deck for enclosed rail-beds. One of the two bridges, Tsing Ma, was planned as the longest suspension bridge in the world. In addition, there would be a new tunnel under Hong Kong's harbor and a continual six-lane access road extending from the airport to Central.

This new airport was meant to show the world that confidence in the future of Hong Kong would be real. This would appear to be in the People's Republic's interest, so it became a valid subject of discussion as to why the PRC would quickly open a new airport in Zhuhai just across from Macau serving eighteen Chinese cities, as well as a new international airport in Macau itself, only 20 miles away from Chep Lap Kok.

Nothing is simple.

THE SECOND SIDE-SHOW: MACAU

One hour away from Hong Kong by hydrofoil (going 40 miles to Hong Kong's northwest) is Macau with its gambling casinos, its tradition of strange things going on, and what used to be its Portuguese Government that had reigned there since 1557. Macau doesn't take up much room.

It, too, would be taken over by the People's Republic of China as a Special Administrative Region. Not on the 1st of July 1997, but on the 20th of December 1999, and the coming takeover was accepted in Macau with a yawn.

No one seemed to care. After all, out of its population of 500,000, 140,000 Macanese were Portuguese passport-holders, and Portugal offered a passport with the "right of abode" to anyone born in Macau before 1981 (anyone who would be 18 or older at the time of the takeover). Ironically enough, they would even have the right to live in Great Britain after European unification, while Hong Kong's British National Overseas passport holders would not have that inherent ability.

China had never been in a hurry to take over Macau, and the Portuguese had not been trying hard to hold on to it. It was the last Portuguese colony, and it was a nuisance. Portugal was willing to give it up in 1975, but Mao Tse-tung and Chou Enlai wanted to wait. They simply weren't ready for it, not quite knowing what to do with it if they had it.

Unlike Hong Kong, Macau had been perceived as merely being under the "caretaker" administration of Portugal at the behest of Beijing, a slice of Chinese territory under an agreed-upon temporary administration of Portugal.

Just like Hong Kong, Macau was also promised 50 years of "a high degree of autonomy" after its handover and could continue the "existing capitalist system and way of life." But since it hadn't been totally autonomous, having been an ally of the PRC even to the point of refusing to accept any of the escaping dissidents from Tiananmen Square (although there were some brave voices of opposition to such a policy among the citizenry, particularly

Reverend Pedro Chung and Ng Kuok Cheong), and since no one was quite sure exactly what system Macau truly would have, few Macau citizens were pressing for guarantees. Only three percent of the population was Portuguese, and with all laws written only in Portuguese, few local Chinese even understood the laws under which they lived. They lived under what was called the "traditional force," which was composed of the main Chinese business communities. Those communities generally sided with Beijing because that is where they made their money.

The casinos would undoubtedly remain (gambling accounted for approximately 40% of the government's revenue), and quite probably Macau would be absorbed into a greater area of China as a suburb of Zhuhai, which was across the border that would soon be erased.

There are indications that Macau could be used by China as a competitor to Hong Kong to keep Hong Kong democracy advocates at bay. With Macau's economy being diversified with textile and garment manufacturing, with a new railway line to Guangzhou, with new land reclamations adding about four square miles to Macau, with a new passenger ferry, with a new deep-water container terminal, and with the ability to compete with Hong Kong's new airport (Macau's new international airport already opened in December of 1995), it certainly appeared that there was a plan enacted to make much more of Macau than it ever had been. The Chinese Government has a long memory and deep wounds. That government well recognized that

Macau was once the most prosperous trading center in the far east—before Hong Kong came along. The People's Republic of China was making a statement to Hong Kong and to the world without saying a word.

14

THE MIDNIGHT OF
BROKEN PROMISES

First, there was the broken promise of the treaty of Nanking signed in 1842, with China ceding Hong Kong Island to Great Britain in *perpetuity* (meaning *forever*) to Great Britain.

The next one came in 1860 with another treaty, this one being the Convention of Peking, with China ceding Kowloon and Stonecutters Island to Great Britain in *perpetuity* (meaning *forever*) to Great Britain.

The third was the agreement in 1898 of China leasing

the New Territories to Great Britain for 99 years, which would come to fruition in 1997 and the only one of the three agreements *not* in *perpetuity* (meaning *not forever*) to Great Britain.

Governor Patten had asked Jack Edwards to deliver to him the Union Jack that had saved Hong Kong during WWII "without any fanfare...Secrecy without flash." Governor Patten then added, "That flag was first up, and it should be last down."

Just as Governor Patten had promised, the flag that was raised on August 19, 1945 on the Peak was raised outside Governor's House on June the 30th of 1997 prior to the coming midnight. It was raised in the rain at 4:30 in the afternoon and just as Governor Patten planned, it was done "without flash," with only family, staff, friends (including Jack Edwards) and tears present.

The depressing event of 1997 was now to be "celebrated," although its planners knew there were no festivities to be celebrated by most Hong Kong people who knew that Hong Kong Island and the Kowloon Peninsula had been the properties of Great Britain forever. The convenient memory loss of most others was often followed by the excuse of "unequal treaties," a phrase invented by Deng Xiaoping as the new explanation when he, "as a compromise," promised Britain's Prime Minister Thatcher there would be "One Country, Two Systems" for fifty years from 1997 forward.

At the event of 1997's June 30th passing to July the First, there were four thousand people who were invited guests from forty-four countries. It seemed as though inside the new extension of Hong Kong's Convention and Exhibition Centre, all of those invited guests were on the escalators at the same time that night. Even though outside there was a heavy rain, most of the crowd was dry since they were coming from the State Banquet in the Centre hosted by Great Britain's Secretary of State for Foreign and Commonwealth Affairs, Robin Cook. Now, however, the invited guests were joined by members of the media from all over the world who were wet and left uncounted. Moreover, at the State Banquet hosted by the British, President Jiang of the People's Republic of China, as well as Premier Li Peng, were not there as they refused the invitation from the British.

The exterior of the building was a cross between the wings of a bird and the sea. Inside, the Grand Hall of the Convention and Exhibition Centre Extension was as magnificent as the exterior of the building. The thousands of invited guests were not only witnesses to history in the handover from Great Britain to the People's Republic of China, but they became the audience of the first event in an architectural wonder of creativity designed and constructed by Hong Kong people.

The Grand Hall of the Convention and Exhibition Center Extension was so massive that nothing was crowded. Just as the exterior of the building was a cross between a bird and the sea, the interior gave the audience the feeling of being beneath the wings of the bird or beneath the breakers of the sea. Although few theaters have windows, to exclude them from this theater would have been criminal. The entire wall behind the stage was glass with intervening blue curtains, the glass exhibiting the magnificence of Victoria Harbor looking toward Kowloon.

On the west side of the stage was Vice-Chairman of the People's Republic of China's Central Military Commission and Chief of the People's Liberation Army General Zhang Wannian, the newly-named Chief Executive of Hong Kong, Tung Chee-hwa, Vice-Premier of the PRC's Qian Qichen, Premier Li Ping, and President Jiang Zemin, who was representing the PRC as the incoming government over Hong Kong. On the east side of the stage was Charles, Prince of Wales, Prime Minister Tony Blair, Foreign Secretary Robin Cook, Governor Christopher Patten, and the Territory's Commander of British Forces Major-General Bryan Dutton, representing the outgoing government of Hong Kong.

Also on the stage were two flag poles on the west side and two flag poles on the east side. The ones to the west were vacant. The ones to the east had the Union Jack and the flag of Hong Kong. The ceiling of the Centre was so high that the flagpoles were full of exterior-length flagpoles with a great quantity of room to spare above them. In addition, there were giant boards with the painted flags of both Great Britain and the People's Republic of China hanging from the ceiling between the stage and the glass wall.

It was time designated to speak for some and the time

to listen for designated others. The voice of Prince Charles was strong and firm and, above all, dignified, as he said:

"Most of all I should like to pay tribute to the people of Hong Kong themselves—to all that they have achieved in the last century and a half. The triumphant success of Hong Kong demands and deserves to be maintained. Hong Kong has shown the world how dynamism and stability can be defining characteristics of a successful society. These have together created a great economy which is the envy of the world. Hong Kong has shown the world how east and west can live and work together...

"Ladies and Gentlemen, China will tonight take responsibility for a place and a people which matter greatly to us all. The solemn pledges made before the world in the 1984 Joint Declaration guarantee the continuity of Hong Kong's way of life. To its part, the United Kingdom will maintain its unwavering support for the Joint Declaration. Our commitment and our strong links to Hong Kong will continue and will—I'm confident—flourish as Hong Kong and its people themselves continue to flourish.

"Distinguished guests, ladies and gentlemen, I should like on behalf of Her Majesty the Queen, and of the entire British people, to express our thanks, admiration, affection, and good wishes to all the people of Hong Kong who have been such staunch and special friends over so many generations. We shall not forget you, and we shall watch with the closest interest as you embark on this new era of your remarkable history."

The timing of the event was run with the precision of a stopwatch. When the Prince of Wales was done, three soldiers of the PRC's People's Liberation Army goose-stepped up the center steps to the red-carpeted stage, with the middle soldier holding the folded flag of the People's Republic of China in his outstretched arms, forming a tray. Then three British soldiers joined them in goose-step. When the delegation of six reached center-stage, five of them saluted the Chinese leaders while the sixth held the flag. Then they separated with the three representing the People's Republic of China marching to a vacant flagpole, and the three representing the British Government marching to the flagpole that was flying the Union Jack of Great Britain.

The flag of the People's Republic of China was then clipped to the rope of that vacant flagpole. The flag was not yet raised.

Then three white-uniformed police of the Hong Kong Special Administrative Region marched up the center steps to the red-carpeted stage, with the middle policeman holding the folded Bauhinia flag of the Hong Kong Special Administrative Region in his outstretched arms, which was forming a tray. Then three Royal Hong Kong police joined them. When the delegation of six reached center-stage, five of them saluted the British leaders while the sixth held the flag. Then they separated, with the three representing the British Government marching to the flagpole flying the flag of Hong Kong, and the three representing the Hong Kong Special Administrative Region marching to the last vacant and unclipped flagpole.

The flag of the Hong Kong Special Administrative Region was then clipped to the rope of that vacant flagpole. It was not raised.

A voice announced, "The Union flag and the Hong Kong flag will now be lowered, and the national flag of the People's Republic of China and the Hong Kong Special Administrative Region flag will be raised." Then the same announcement was made in Cantonese.

As the Union Jack and Hong Kong flags were lowered simultaneously, the orchestra played "God Save the Queen." Prince Charles and Governor Patten, two strong men, were trying unsuccessfully to hold back tears, as were the others in the British delegation on stage.

There wasn't a citizen of Great Britain in the audience that wasn't crying. And so were most of the Hong Kong people who attended. And so were most of the Americans there. And so were many from Hong Kong and others outside of the Center.

When the orchestra was done, there were only fifteen seconds left until midnight. For fifteen seconds, there was silence interrupted by sniffing and little else.

Midnight.

The flags of the People's Republic of China and the

Bauhinia flag of the Hong Kong Special Administrative Region were raised simultaneously as the orchestra played the National Anthem of the People's Republic of China.

It was done.

A cable written previously at Government House was sent two seconds past midnight to the United Kingdom's Secretary of State: "I have relinquished the administration of this government. God Save the Queen. Patten."

The guests went to one of three major destinations. The chief destination of Americans was to go to their hotels and get out of the public spotlight, following the lead of U.S. Secretary of State Albright. As the highest representative of the U.S. Government, she went to the Handover Ceremonies but was boycotting the inauguration of the Provisional Legislature up the escalator from the Grand Hall. That destination was a protocol duty of the United States Consul General in Hong Kong who was Richard Boucher, who knew he was being used as a representative of the U.S. so that the inauguration would not be a total snub by the U.S. Government. British Prime Minister Tony Blair boycotted the inaugural and sent Great Britain's Senior Representative to the Sino-British Liaison Group, Hugh Davies, and sent Consul General in Hong Kong, Francis Cornish. Clearly, Richard Boucher, Hugh Davies, and Francis Cornish would rather not have attended, preferring to be at the third possible destination.

That third possible destination was the one favored by those guests who were proud to publicly exhibit their preference for Great Britain over the People's Republic of China by going to East Tamar Naval Base where the Royal Yacht Britannia, an honor guard, and three British naval vessels bathed in white lights, were waiting for the Prince of Wales and for Governor Patten and his family.

It was a five-minute ride of the motorcade from the Convention and Exhibition Center to arrive at East Tamar. Waiting was a crowd of thousands of Hong Kong people. Helicopters were circling overhead. Just above the crowds, below the helicopters, and above the ships were many low and dark clouds, but those clouds disciplined themselves not to break and cause rain during the departure of the British delegation.

There was waving and tears from the Royal Yacht Britannia and waving and tears from the crowd.

At 12:40 A.M. the Britannia's engines started. Then the Britannia left the pier for its last official voyage before being decommissioned.

"Rule Britannia!" Jack Edwards yelled at the departing ship. And then others yelled, "Rule Britannia!" as well. For the rest of the crowd, some added another yell of "Rule Britannia!" Then there was silence. In a short time, the silence became unendurably long.

For those not there but watching the events on television or listening to them on radio, many heard the painful words, "We are broadcasting from Hong Kong, a SAR; a Special Administrative Region of the People's Republic of China."

15

HONG KONG
WITHOUT A NET

On the first day of the take-over on the 1st of July 1997, the office of Governor of Hong Kong as sent by London was to be over and done and replaced by Beijing with the highest office in residence, and to be not titled Governor but the Office of Chief Executive. By the 1st of July 2017, holding that title was Carrie Lam, a citizen of Hong Kong but politically favored by the People's Republic of China and known to have been elected by the winning amount of votes of the Election Committee of the Central Committee of the People's Republic of China's Government in Beijing.

There were demonstrations by Hong Kong people against her assuming that position. Those demonstrations had become routine in March of 2019 for any number of her decisions. The demonstrations turned massive on the 9th of June 2019 when she made a decision that was no surprise but tremendously opposed by thousands of Hong Kong people that filled parts of the Central area of Hong Kong Island: She favored a law that a Hong Kong citizen suspected of a crime should be extradited from Hong Kong to Beijing under the People's Republic of China's laws regarding trial, and if that person should be determined to be guilty, he or she would be subject to punishment as ordered by the People's Republic of China. This was scheduled to come up in Hong Kong's Legislative Council and was already known to be strongly endorsed by the leader of the People's Republic of China, Xi Jinping. It was also known that when he wanted something done in Hong Kong, he would have no serious long-term difficulty in convincing Carrie Lam to support that decision.

As the months went on and Hong Kong's demonstrations against the PRC's directive went on, the size and seriousness of those Hong Kong protests magnified. On Sunday, August the 18th, the participants of the protest reached more than 1.7 million people.

Carrie Lam suspended the bill for extradition, but that did not meet all the protestor's pleas:

Number One in that list was not to just *suspend* the

Extradition Bill but to *withdraw* it entirely.

Number Two was to have an independent inquiry of police brutality that was acting against demonstrators.

Number Three was to release protestors under arrest.

Number Four was the withdrawal of the accusation of riot charges of demonstrators participating in the June 12 and June 15 protests.

Number Five was to have Universal Suffrage in elections.

"Please Help" signs were now carried by those outside the U.S. Consulate. Those signs were held beneath U.S. flags being respectfully waived by demonstrators beyond the Consulate. Another demonstration was then held on Monday, the 19th of August, where there was a huge demonstration in Victoria Park where Hong Kong police estimated there were 128,000 demonstrators with over 700 of them arrested, many charged with rioting. It had been the day before then (August the 18th) when President of the United States Donald Trump had said, "Two weeks ago, they've (Hong Kong) had riots for a long period, and I don't know what China's attitude is. Somebody said that, at some point, they're going to want to stop that. But that's between Hong Kong and China because Hong Kong is part of China. They have to deal with that themselves." (No, it isn't part of China because they gave Hong Kong Island up in 1841/1842 in perpetuity to Great Britain and gave Kowloon to Great Britain in perpetuity in 1860.) And for those who argue that those 19th Century agreements were a long time ago so should no longer be observed, it should be kept in mind that in 2076 it will be the U.S.'s Tri-Centennial celebration of the victory of the United States in its Revolutionary War against Great Britain, and no one expects Great Britain to demand the U.S. territory now be given back to Great Britain since the U.S. victory was a long time ago. A nation's word should be a nation's word.

The newer 2019 decision of Xi to demand the extradition of Hong Kong citizens to Beijing starting in 2019 was an action he took against all international protocol and against the code of traditional diplomacy and against the will of Hong Kong people who did not elect either Xi Jinping or Carrie Lam and, to be brief, it was against the PRC's word. It should not have surprised anyone, since a habit of non-democracies is to use an international agreement, not for a guarantee to the other party, but for a device to bring about its deception in hidden purposes yet to become known.

On September the 4th, Item Number One of the protestor's pleas was to exchange the word "suspend" to "withdraw" the bill for extradition to the People's Republic of China. On that day, Chief Executive Carrie Lam did exactly that. Doing it probably took courage and guts, with her position as Chief Executive now being likely to be temporary at best under the PRC's President Xi Jinping.

Chief Executive Carrie Lam gave no response on the other four pleas of demonstrators who, in mass, respectfully called for a strong statement by the United States, but it hadn't yet come. Over 100,000 peacefully demonstrated outside the U.S. Consulate requesting the U.S. Congress pass the Hong Kong Human Rights and Democracy act that had been proposed in 2017, with what appeared to have bipartisan support, but it had still not passed.

From the United States, President Trump tweeted that: "I know President Xi well. He is a great leader. If President Xi would meet directly and personally with the protestors' leaders, it would be a happy and enlightened meeting."

It was a hypothetical scenario, since it was most likely that Xi Jinping would come to Hong Kong for such a meeting, and it would be too much risk to the protestors' leaders for them to be in Beijing for any purpose. The best idea would have been for the United States to support the protestors in their five pleas until those pleas were granted. That didn't seem to be the policy. At least not yet.

Mahatma Gandhi was once asked what he thought of western civilization and he answered, "I think it would be a good idea." He was right. It would be.

16

A LANDSLIDE FOR LIBERTY ON MORE THAN ONE THANKSGIVING

It had been common in the United States to see television-news of foreign countries showing U.S. Flags being burned in Anti-U.S. demonstrations, often taking place on streets in Iran or in streets run by other governments that are hostile to the United States, or even the burning flags of nations friendly to the United States.

It became a different world close to and on the U.S.'s

Thanksgiving Day of 2019, when television sets and press photos were seen in newscasts exhibiting thousands of people in Hong Kong waving U.S. flags, with voices of those crowds shouting messages of appreciation and gratitude for the support of the United States in Hong Kong's quest to retain the liberties with which they had continued to live for so many years, rather than to accept the domination of laws and obedience to the government of the People's Republic of China. Suddenly from those demonstrators came the voices of Hong Kong people singing the Nation Anthem of the United States in thanks for the support of the U.S.

A short chronology of Thanksgiving Day and surrounding days follows:

Sunday, 11-24-19—Ballots were cast in a landslide for liberty by the Hong Kong people. The most frequent description of such election results by the worldwide press were "landslide" and "unprecedented" and "unpredicted." 452 seats of the 18 District Councils were on ballots in races deciding 18 District Councils. 17 of those 18 councils have now become pro-democracy by the count of ballot results.

Tuesday, 11-26-19—Support was received for H.R. 3289 of the U.S. House of Representatives and S. 1838 of the U.S. Senate. (Both Bills were Pro-Liberty support for Hong Kong and that legislation was sent to the White House for the President's decision of whether or not to sign the bills; his signature meant the legislation would then become laws of the United States calling for sanctions on those who commit human rights abuses against Hong Kong people.)

There were quick warnings from the People's Republic of China's President Xi Jinping: "The United States has committed a nakedly hegemonic act" and "Firm counter-measures will be taken."

It is unanswerable to know why the PRC's leaders since 1949's Mao Tse-tung all the way to the current leadership of Xi Jinping have chosen to capture, incarcerate, torture, and murder millions of their own Chinese people, and certainly have maintained more faith and belief in themselves than in their nation's own citizens—and, for sure, in credit to the United States and some other democracies of the world, which have cared more about the human rights of the Chinese people than all of those leaders of the People's Republic of China chose to pursue through the seventy years of their PRC leadership.

Wednesday, 11-27-19—The legislation entitled "Hong Kong Human Rights and Democracy Act of 2019" was signed by U.S. President Trump. From his signature forward meant, among other things, that Hong Kong would be treated autonomously by the United States, including having trading advantages. The law required the U.S. State Department to give annual certifications that Hong Kong was free enough to have and retain such individual rights. The legislation noted that Hong Kong had formally been part of the United Kingdom for about 150 years and "China has ramped up control since 1997," further noting that "This summer's proposed bill in Hong Kong about extraditions—which would make it easier for their citizens accused of a crime to be sent away, including most notably to mainland China where dissidents can be 'disappeared'" was seen by many in Hong Kong as the last straw...The United States Hong Kong Act of 1992 has governed U.S. policy toward the region. Essentially, that maintains all treaties and commitments to Hong Kong regardless of China's official national agreement or participation. China, of course, criticized the legislation at the time of its enactment.

The Hong Kong Rights and Democracy Act required that the State Department re-certify Hong Kong's autonomous nature in order for the so-called 'special treatment' the U.S. affords Hong Kong to continue. It would also mandate the U.S. government to identify any specific people involved in abductions of Hong Kong protesters or extraditions of Hong Kong citizens to mainland China, and freeze any of their U.S. based assets and deny them physical entry into the U.S. Lastly, it clarifies under federal law that nobody should be denied a visa to the U.S. on the basis of participating in Hong Kong protests.

As written:

> "Supporters agree that the legislation stands on the side of human rights, democracy, and personal freedom over autocracy, government control, and authoritarianism…

> "As over one million Hong Kongers take to the streets protesting amendments to the territory's extradition law, the U.S. must send a strong message that we stand with those peacefully advocating for freedom and the rule of law and against Beijing's growing interference in Hong Kong's affairs."

Thursday, Thanksgiving, 11-28-19—Rallies of thousands of Hong Kong people thanked the United States for its support with the leading statement of "The rationale for us having this rally is to show our gratitude and thank the United States Congress and President Trump for passing the bill."

Friday, 11-29-19—Hong Kong celebrations continue with crowds waving U.S. Flags and statements made to the world press.

For those old enough to remember, these celebrations of Hong Kong were similar to the celebrations of the victors of 1945's V-E Day when Nazi Germany was defeated in World War II and 1945's V-J Day for the allies' success over the end of Japan's Empire during World War II. The new Thanksgiving Hong Kong celebrations were commensurate with the destruction of the Berlin Wall in 1989. It was the "Dot-Dot-Dot Dash" of Beethoven's Fifth Symphony and its accompanying message of victory for human rights.

Saturday, 11-30-19 through the 2nd of December 2019—Demonstrations of Thanksgiving continuing throughout Hong Kong. Also continued were threats by Xi Jinping leveled against the United States. On the 2nd of December, he gave the statement that ''the People's Republic of China is suspending any U.S. military personnel from entering Hong Kong" ... and President Xi gave more warnings of "counter-measures" to come against the United States. But the images of thousands of Hong Kong people waving U.S. Flags and singing the Star-Spangled Banner, the U.S.'s National Anthem, and shouting their thanks to the United States took Thanksgiving precedence, giving a memory providing an example of how to treat a friend.

17

TIMES AHEAD

TIMES AHEAD THOUGHT TO BE FOR THE PRESIDENCY

Within the White House, there was and perhaps still is a volume of the Inaugural Addresses of the Presidents of the United States resting in the bookshelf in front of the west wall of the Oval Office. If that book was not removed by 2019, it would still have the phrase within the text of the 1961 Inaugural Address of President John F. Kennedy that reads: *"Let every nation know, whether it wishes us well or ill, that we shall pay any price, bear any burden, meet any hardship, support any friend, oppose any foe to assure the survival and the success of liberty.*"Maybe, just maybe, those words were read in the year 2019 from that copy of the volume because there was the action of President Trump to do for Hong Kong people what President Kennedy articulated for the United States in his Inaugural Address fifty-eight years before.

At the time of our next Presidential Inauguration, it might be vital to include a statement regarding the expectation of our nation that Hong Kong Island's and Kowloon's citizens will be allowed to live by their own laws in perpetuity as promised by China in the 1800s.

TIMES AHEAD THOUGHT TO BE FOR THE U.S. DEPARTMENT OF DEFENSE

When the PRC claimed sovereignty of the Spratly Islands, contested by the Philippines, Vietnam, Brunei, Malaysia, and Taiwan, and when the PRC seized the ninth Spratly Island, we issued no challenge at all. Secretary of State James Baker had said nothing when the dispute over the seventh and eighth islands had erupted. Later, neither had Secretary Warren Christopher said anything regarding the ninth island seized. Admiral Richard Macke, the Commander of U.S. Forces in the Pacific, said, "What we have to do is make China one of our friends. We can't confront them... We don't need a security treaty or anything like that with China." The last sentence was the only one that was right, since their signature on a document of peace is meaningless.

A future military alliance between the People's Republic of China and the Islamic Fundamentalist Revolution over a seemingly unrelated dispute such as Kashmir could cause a global axis involving over half the peoples of the world.

TIMES AHEAD THOUGHT TO BE FOR U.S. NAVY: ESTABLISH THE UNITED STATES' CONTINUING RIGHT OF PORT CALLS

There were regularly some 50 to 70 U.S. Naval port calls a year in Hong Kong. Does Article 126 of the Basic Law mean that permission must be first obtained from Beijing? Article 126 of the Basic Law states, "With the exception of foreign warships, access for which requires the special permission of the Central People's Government, ships shall enjoy access to the ports of the Hong Kong Special Administrative Region in accordance with the laws of the Region." (The Joint Declaration also cites the "exception of foreign warships" in Annex I, Part 8). Our continuing right must be established. To simply assume that the right continues in the eyes of the PRC without questioning could suggest we are afraid to ask. They should be afraid of our questions regarding the new laws they have set into writing in Hong Kong's Basic Law.

TIMES AHEAD THOUGHT TO BE FOR THE U.S. DEPARTMENT OF STATE

As defined by the U.S. State Department, The United States has a two-track policy toward the People's Republic of China: one track heading toward economic stability and western investment in the PRC, and the other track for progress in human rights and civil liberties in the PRC. There is nothing wrong with the tracks; it's the trains. The

Economic Amtrak leaves the station every twenty minutes—while seeing or hearing the sound of a Human Rights
Express causes an argument every time it leaves the station.

Since the 15th of December 1978, when President Carter
announced diplomatic recognition of the People's Republic
of China (breaking relations with the Republic of China on
Taiwan, removing all U.S. military forces from Taiwan, and
abrogating the U.S.'s Mutual Defense Treaty of 1954 with
the Republic on Taiwan), the disagreements between our two
nations have, with little exception, been concluded in favor
of the position of the People's Republic of China.

Until June of 1994, there was at least a Civil Liberties
Car on the Economic train, but that car was "de-linked"
by President Clinton when Most Favored Nation Status
was granted to the People's Republic of China without
the attachment of human rights. To the applause of some
investors in China, he said that de-linking human rights
from trade "offers us the best opportunity to lay the basis
for long-term sustainable progress on human rights and for
the advancement of our other interests with China."

Some of them, certainly not all, but some of them
applauded because the President's statement gave a moral
justification to consistently referring to one billion customers. With courage, some who were there instead referred
to one billion human beings, not customers.

Prior to United States involvement in World War II,
there was a book entitled *You Can't Do Business with Hitler*.
It was authored by Douglas Miller. No need for a summary

here; the title is its summary. The book was ridiculed at worst and ignored at best by many who, in fact, allowed the Nazis to build a first-class military. *You Can't Do Business with Hitler* was not a best-seller. Neither would a current book entitled *You Can't Do Business with Xi Jinping.*

For sure, the U.S. Department of State should establish the continuing right of visiting officials of the United States and the right of other U.S. visitors to Hong Kong even if deemed politically unacceptable to the PRC. It should be clear that control over Hong Kong's foreign affairs is not a matter for the PRC and that members of the United States Congress and other U.S. officials visiting Hong Kong need not first obtain the sanction of Beijing. U.S. citizens previously judged unacceptable for political reasons to visit the People's Republic of China should not be made unacceptable to visit Hong Kong. The continuation of U.S. rights should be unmistakably established.

TIMES AHEAD FOR U.S. TOURISTS AND OTHER U.S. CITIZENS IN FOREIGN COUNTRIES

You shouldn't expect to be treated with the same depth of appreciation and respect that U.S. visitors were treated with years back when they cherished the U.S, fighting for their liberty, and where it was common for an American to be embraced on foreign streets by foreign strangers; some crying of joy, not because they knew anything about you other than knowing you were an American, probably because of your clothes or voice or something else that only foreigners could use as a credible recognizer. "And please thank your friends, your people, your president, for us, for what America does to make our nation be free again! Thank you for being an American!" And after parting, it was common to brush the shoulder of your jacket and feel that it was still moist from tears left on it from that crying embrace of a stranger.

Of course, such an episode won't happen anymore if the United States' decision is to adopt an isolationist policy rather than have the U.S. military fight "endless wars that last forever and ever and ever and cost millions and billions of dollars." That quote would assume we had the U.S. military only fighting in wars, whereas most of the military, so accused, had been preserving the peace that we gained by having fought in those wars until the opposition surrendered. As for the money we spend on those engagements, that statement assumes the lives of foreigners are not worth the money to save them.

It has been recently stated that we should stay home and only defend our own people and let others from other nations fight for themselves. Putting all this into something personal: if you were walking on a night-street and saw a loved one or friend being accosted by a large gang, way beyond your single physical means to rescue your loved one or your friend, would you get the police or others or both to help you perform the rescue the victim needed? If you would, instead, quickly walk away so as to escape the situation—if that be the case, if that should happen, the one you leave to the gang should dump you immediately if that person is still alive.

Extending this to particular foreign engagements in terms of 2019, the new proposal for an agreement between the U.S. and the Taliban of Afghanistan is absurd, unless we don't care that the Taliban had instituted that the public of Afghanistan attend their ceremonies on weekends outside their "Justice Department," where women were brought into the outdoor stadium in wagons having been tied together, and then let out of the wagons for the crowds to throw rocks and bricks at them until they were dead. Their crimes were learning from books or being seen with a man, both walking together.

The Taliban is a living example of governmental evil.

TO REMEMBER: THE U.S. AFFILIATION WITH HONG KONG FROM THE U.S. LAWS OF 1992 THROUGH 2019

In 1996, The 102nd Congress passed and President George H.W. Bush signed the United States-Hong Kong Policy Act of 1992 that established United States recognition that Hong Kong will be dealt with as the autonomous region agreed upon in the Joint Declaration and Basic Law, and the 1992 act established that all previous agreements with Hong Kong will remain in full force, and the U.S. will treat Hong Kong as a separate and distinct entity. The Act also emphasized our support for democratization and human rights. It was an excellent act of Congress and the fact that it passed and was signed by the President and stands now even more forceful and more current, since the signing of the 2019 laws of the United States. Realistically, however, acts of law of previous times have a limited shelf-life in terms of influencing all parties involved. Re-statements by current Administrations and Congress can sometimes be essential to prevent others from believing the issue has run its course and is done. If our often-discarded laws of 1992 and our more current laws of 2019 are not observed in totality, there must be a re-emphasis dependent on world events, particularly from threats and possible actions by Xi Jinping.

TIMES PREDICTED FOR HONG KONG'S RIGHT OF SECOND ABODE

It remains in Great Britain's hands: Governor Chris Patten had advocated that Great Britain give the "right of abode" to all Hong Kong people qualifying for British Passports. (3.3 million.) His government immediately rejected his proposal. Governor Patten said that no one seriously believes that three million citizens would actually leave Hong Kong if they had the "right of abode." Without saying it, his advocacy was obviously meant to be a disincentive for the People's Republic of China to impose any strangulation of Hong Kong's liberties. It would be far more difficult to abrogate civil liberties from those who could live elsewhere rather than only from those who had no choice but to stay in Hong Kong. If our influence is intact, we should propose that "First Abode" be given for a designated period of something appropriate, such as one or two years to those using their passports to leave Hong Kong to go to Great Britain, requiring that they become constructive members of their society during that period of time. After that, if Great

Britain so chooses, they could, of course, give the visitor a more permanent residence or send them back to Hong Kong, assuming Hong Kong would still have the right to reject them coming back.

18

WHAT THE PRC DID TO HONG KONG IN 1997 IS LIKELY TO BE WHAT THE PRC WILL DO TO TAIWAN BY OR IN 2047

The government of the People's Republic of China has claimed possession of Taiwan since the PRC came into power on the 1st of October 1949. It is true that during different periods of history Taiwan has been under the jurisdiction of the Emperor of China and the Republic of China (ROC). But it has also been under the jurisdiction of Portugal, the Netherlands, Spain, Japan, and more recently by its own population as a democracy. It has never, not even for a minute, been under the jurisdiction of the People's Republic of China. That flag has never been raised over Taiwan. That name has never been adopted in Taiwan. That government has never been accepted in Taiwan. That system has never been established in Taiwan. Yet the government of the People's Republic of China refers to Taiwan as its "renegade province," which it will take by "non-peaceful means" if necessary.

It would make more sense for Great Britain's prime minister to claim the United States of America as a renegade province of the United Kingdom. With even greater logic, Japan's prime minister could make the claim that Taiwan is a renegade province of Japan since Japan was granted possession of Taiwan in perpetuity by China in the 1895 Treaty of Shimonoseki. (It was signed by the plenipotentiary Li Hung-chang for the Emperor of China.) Japan held Taiwan for fifty years, from 1895 until 1945, when World War II ended and did not officially surrender Taiwan until the 8th of September 1951, when its representatives signed the San Francisco Peace Treaty.

Chapter II, Article 2 of that Treaty stated, "Japan renounces all right, title, and claim to Formosa [the Portuguese name for Taiwan] and the Pescadores [islands]." Note that Japan renounced its jurisdiction of Taiwan but did not surrender Taiwan to any particular power.

Since it began in 1949, the government of the People's Republic of China has suffered under the disability of three obsessions:

1. The lust for governmental control.

2. The policy that China's treaties and agreements made prior to the communist revolution has no continuing authority, while any territory they regard as a possession during pre-revolution China must obey China's current authority.

3. The belief that China's unelected government is superior to giving the choice of leaders to those governed: the people of China or the people of any place they consider to be part of China.

After Great Britain's 1997 handover of Hong Kong to the government of the People's Republic of China and, to a lesser extent, Portugal's 1999 handover of Macau to the PRC government, all three obsessions have been targeted at Taiwan for which the PRC has long proclaimed what they call "The Three No's":

1. No independence of Taiwan.

2. No acceptance of diplomatic relations with any government that proclaims there are two Chinas, or one China and one Taiwan.

3. No acceptance of Taiwan into any international organization as a separate state.

On the 9th of July 1999, President Lee of Taiwan used three words that created a firestorm. In a radio interview with Deutsche Welle ("Voice of Germany"), President Lee said that any talks between China and Taiwan should be conducted on a "state-to-state" relationship. The People's Republic of China quickly warned of military intervention against Taiwan. The Clinton administration in the U.S. was up in arms over President Lee's statement, and President Lee's political party, the Kuomintang, made futile attempts to soften what President Lee had said.

The PRC's minister of defense, Chi Haotian, said that the army "is ready at any time to safeguard the territorial integrity of China and smash any attempts to separate the country."

President Clinton phoned China's president Jiang Zemin to assure him that the United States retained a "one China" policy.

The spokesman for the Ministry of Foreign Affairs in Beijing, Zhu Bangzao, said:

> "We hereby warn Lee Teng-hui and the Taiwan authorities not to underestimate the firm resolve of the Chinese government to safeguard the sovereignty, dignity, and territorial integrity of the courage and strength of the Chinese people to fight against separation and Taiwan's independence. The reunification of China represents the general trend and the popular will. Lee Teng-hui and Taiwan authorities should size up the situation soberly, rein in at the brink of the precipice, and immediately cease all separatist activities."

Beyond threats, the People's Republic of China used the weapon of international humiliation against Taiwan. Beijing has pressured the World Trade Organization not to give any official titles to representatives from Taiwan and insists that the World Trade Organization's directory refer to them only as "Mr." and "Ms." rather than any national title. Taiwan wanted to join the Association of Southeast Asian Nations (ASEAN) and was invited to join in 1991 with a precondition stipulated by Beijing. Its membership had to be under the name of Chinese Taipei, or it would be unable to join. In order to participate in the Olympic Games, the same designation of Chinese Taipei is required, with the rule that Taiwan cannot have its national anthem played, nor is the display of Taiwan's flag permitted.

Under pressure from his own political party, the Kuomintang that was winking at the PRC, Taiwan's President Lee Teng-hui finally had it and split from the Kuomintang political party in 2000, as the Kuomintang was changing policies even further toward the People's Republic of China into friendly relationships, increased trade, acceptance of humiliations, and pacifying statements. President Lee warned the Kuomintang that their extended hand would eventually be turned into aggression against Taiwan by China.

The Democratic Progressive Party (DPP) that had been born illegally in 1986 expanded in popularity and won the presidential vote of 2000 with the election of President Chen Shui-bian and Vice President Annette Hsiu-lien Lu.

For the first time since China reclaimed Taiwan after World War II (held by Japan since 1895), the Kuomintang was out of presidential power.

When Deng Xiaoping met with Prime Minister Thatcher of Great Britain, he agreed to allow Hong Kong to retain its own system for the next fifty years, until 2047, and "One Country, Two Systems" was the way he defined it. The error of that definition was that the two systems were decreed as communism for the mainland and capitalism for Hong Kong.

But the system of the mainland was fascism, and the system of Hong Kong was liberty. On mainland China, many large urban areas were highly capitalistic at the time of handover—but the people did not live in liberty. Capitalism is nothing more or less than the economic dimension of liberty, but not the only element. It is for sure that people cannot be free without capitalism, but it is possible to have capitalism and not be free, as has been proven by so many fascist governments. And that is just the way the government of the People's Republic of China wants it: a dictatorship that exalts one party, one government, and one race.

It so happened that the phrase "One Country, Two Systems" was inaugurated in Hong Kong on the midnight that separated June the 30th from July the 1st of 1997. Prior to the prescribed handover, Tung Cheehwa was "elected" Hong Kong's chief executive to take office for five years starting at the moment of jurisdiction by the People's Republic of China.

His election was decided by an Election Committee of four hundred who were chosen by the Preparatory Committee, which was chosen by Beijing. On handover night, Jiang Zemin, the president of the People's Republic of China at the time, talked of the shame and humiliation that China had suffered because of the Opium Wars and Great Britain's jurisdiction of Hong Kong for so many years. However, the real humiliation suffered by Jiang Zemin was the evidence on constant display to the world of what Chinese people could do without the government of the People's Republic of China. There was no contest between Hong Kong and any city under the domination of the People's Republic. The shame and humiliation were due to the success of the Chinese people who fled to Hong Kong, rejecting the government of the People's Republic of China.

During that evening, political cracks appeared in the foundation of Hong Kong. Since then, those cracks have widened and deepened and spread further apart, intentionally by the PRC. What was not part of the midnight ceremony was any mention of the changes in the laws that governed Hong Kong; the changes coming from "one country, two systems." Those changes are worthy of notice by the advocates of the People's Republic of China's offer to Taiwan of having "one country, two systems" for itself as Hong Kong now had, but on the 30th of June, Hong Kong's Bill of Rights was in full force, while on the 1st of July important provisions to that Bill of Rights were thrown out. To the detriment of Hong Kong and to the benefit of Taiwan, an example of "one country, two systems" has been established. Since the 1997 handover, Hong Kong has progressively become less and less unique. Not visually. To the tourist, the businessperson, and most travelers, the changes in Hong Kong are not obvious. The skyline remains spectacular, the hotels are still luxurious, the streets are as crowded as ever, and the shopping centers are unmanageably chaotic. The visuals are still magnificent, while most visitors have no way to know the chronology of the invisible. Anson Chan had warned that Hong Kong could become "just another Chinese city." Not yet. But close.

Knowing what we have seen in the years since the handover, "one country, two systems" has become, as predicted by Law Yuk-kai, the "frog over a gentle fire," with the temperature rising. And there is the unanswered question: Why was there a time limit specified for the "one country, two systems" status of Hong Kong? What is supposed to happen in the termination year of 2047?

No need to dwell on it. Taiwan is perceived to be in the crosshairs by 2047 with, by then, Hong Kong living under the control of the PRC in the concept they call beyond the hearing of others, "Shhhh: One Country, One System."

19

NOLA

How will the Hong Kong people live in the years ahead? With hope, the People's Republic of China will be out of the domination picture. If not, and if it chooses to rule Hong Kong, the People's Republic of China would then win militarily, because even if Hong Kong wouldn't be won by the PRC's invasion, the PRC could win simply by delivering the issue to the Security Council of the United Nations. That would immediately mean there would be no contest at all: Since the People's Republic of China has a permanent seat in the Security Council, the PRC could and would veto any win for the Hong Kong people. That would mean that

Hong Kong people would immediately be answerable to the laws of the PRC. (The original five Security Council members were five victors of World War II: The USA, Great Britain, France, the Soviet Union—*not Russia*—and the *Republic* of China—*not* the *People's* Republic of China.)

It is important for Hong Kong people to never sign anything giving one inch to a representative of the PRC, and not to agree to have any issue come up in the UN's Security Council regarding Hong Kong—or even in the UN's General Assembly—without a fight. It is also important for any nation to know and important for any interested observer to know that the United Nations organization has long been of infinitely more value to the PRC than it has been to free nations of the world. The UN continues to give rewards to inheritors of nation's victories in World War II when World War II is no longer the criterion that should be used, with world events having graduated from 1945 into current dates and events.

If the reader is an American, imagine that you and your family move to a new home in a neighborhood of 190 other residences. As you carry in some of your possessions, you are welcomed outside your front door by the Chairman of the Neighborhood Community Services Organization. He extends his hand and introduces himself and says, "Welcome! We have 190 members in our Neighborhood Community Services, and we would like to have you in our organization as our 191st member! We had a meeting last night, and all of your neighbors would like you to join. Our members are diverse. Some of them are murderers, kidnappers, hostage-takers, and slave-masters. But not all of them! And because you have such a nice house—really the nicest house in the neighborhood—our members expect you to pay 22% of our budget. In short, be our prime benefactor. Your home exhibits that you can afford it." Would you join? Would you want to be in a club with those members? Would you want to regularly sit next to them?

Whether you know it or not, all U.S. citizens and other representatives from other free nations sit next to them. It isn't called the Neighborhood Community Services Organization. It's called the United Nations.

To ensure that these kinds of totalitarian vs. democracy battles end, the U.S. should initiate a new kind of international organization to replace the U.N.

It was in the middle of the 1970s that the late Daniel Moynihan entered and exited as the U.S. Ambassador to the United Nations. Upon leaving that post, he gave three definitions of the United Nations: "A theater of the absurd, a decomposing corpse, and an insane asylum." Then, giving his remarks support, he quoted a leading British journalist of the time who said that the U.N. was among "the most corrupt and corrupting creations in the whole history of human institutions."

The 1970s were not good years to be a U.S. Ambassador to the U.N. In fact, none of the years of the Cold War were good years to be the U.S. Ambassador to the U.N., as a coalition had formed between the Soviet Union, its satellites, and nations that comprised what were called the U.N.'s "Group of 77" which grew to a membership of 128. Most members of the "Group of 77" were not enamored with the Soviet Union, but they feared the consequences of opposing that government's interests. Their votes in the U.N. eventually took the side of the Soviet Union 99.36% of the time.

Even the United Nations Children's Emergency Fund (UNICEF), financed in large part by U.S. purchasers of UNICEF's Christmas Cards, were charged with sending millions of dollars in aid to North Vietnam during the last year of its war against South Vietnam. UNICEF's spokesman responded, "UNICEF has no way to make sure the supplies got to the children. They were dropped off at the airports and docks, and we assume they were used as we intended." Even if they did get to the children, what UNICEF had dropped off at the airports and docks were not crayons, dolls, and lollipops. They dropped off trucks, bulldozers, and heavy construction material.

In the 1980s, another U.S. Ambassador to the United Nations, Jeane Kirkpatrick, said, "Rather frequently, what goes on in the U.N. actually exacerbates conflicts rather than tending to resolve them."

Those were the days when the U.N. debated the threat posed not by 14 concurrent Soviet proxy wars, and not by Fidel Castro's 40,000 troops on the African Continent, but by U.S. forces in the U.S. Virgin Islands since 14 U.S. Coast Guardsmen were stationed there.

Even during the last full year before the Berlin Wall

came down, the U.N. was the last to give up. That was when the majority of the entire General Assembly voted with the Soviet Union 95.16% of the time.

But time has passed, and the Soviet Union is gone, its empire has dismembered, and the Cold War was won, no thanks to the U.N. that supported what that organization called Wars of National Liberation, which was a diplomat's synonym for wars supported by the Soviet Union.

With the fall of the Soviet Empire and the dismemberment of the Soviet Union, there emerged some hope for the United Nations. Without the power and fear of that state, third world governments ("The Group of 77" with 128 members) were no longer intimidated into a voting pattern by Moscow. It was a time of great potential promise.

The promise was dumped.

The U.N. should have been buried with the Soviet Union, but it survived, looking in new directions. The 1990s brought Secretary-General Boutros Boutros-Ghali's quest for what he called United Nations "empowerment" with an expanding standing army and the ability to collect direct taxes. He made a case in his book, *Agenda for Peace*, that, "It is the task of leaders of States to understand that the time of absolute and exclusive sovereignty, however, has passed." Combined with those beliefs and quests was a Human Rights Conference that changed the meaning of human rights of the people into economic demands of dictatorships. The Conference mandated an "inalienable right" to economic development of poorer nations. The

Human Rights Conference decided that personal liberties could not be itemized since "cultural differences" meant "different things for different nations" and "western definitions" could not apply.

The U.N. grabbed more and larger responsibilities as the United States, in those years, more often felt obliged to work through that organization rather than take action independently or in bilateral or multinational agreements separate and apart from the U.N.

Secretary-General Boutros Boutros-Ghali warned the United States that under existing Security Council resolutions, only he had the power to order the launch of air strikes against the Serbian aggressors fighting Bosnians, and the United States would be in violation of the U.N. Charter if the U.S. acted on its own.

For a long while, the U.S. didn't. Instead, many government diplomats listened and obeyed the head of an organization that included those many unrepentant kidnappers, thieves, murderers, and a new coalition of international terrorists.

Like the League of Nations, the major fault of the U.N. has been more than an individual: It has been and remains a structure. That structure was built with a framework of equivalence between authoritarian dictatorships and democracies.

Ironically, the U.N.'s Charter starts with a bit of plagiarism from the United States Constitution. Instead of "We the people of the United States," it reads, "We the peoples of the United Nations." But, the United Nations has nothing

to do with "We the peoples," but rather, "We the governments, whether or not we were chosen by the people of our
nations." And most weren't.

Beyond that error of organization was another error that
guaranteed the failure of both the League of Nations and
the United Nations, both having had peace as their purpose
rather than liberty. Any negotiator between warring parties
recognizes that peace is easier to achieve by forsaking the
liberties of the people on one side than by resisting masters
on the other side. Any world organization, minimal or
all-encompassing, is bound to be a source of harm rather
than benefit if the authors of its document of purpose fail
to recognize that liberty without peace still has hope, while
peace without liberty is surrender.

The Covenant of the League started by stating its purpose in a long and rambling sentence that made not one
mention of liberty:

> The High Contracting Parties, in order to promote inter-
> national cooperation and to achieve international peace
> and security by the acceptance of obligations not to resort
> to war, by the prescription of open, just and honorable
> relations between nations, by the firm establishment of the
> understandings of international law as the actual rule of
> conduct among governments, and by the maintenance of
> justice and scrupulous respect for all treaty obligations in
> the dealings of organized peoples with one another, agree
> to this Covenant of the League of Nations."

The authors of the Charter of the United Nations wrote a more direct sentence than the message of their predecessors, but it was also devoid of the word "liberty." Chapter 1, Article 1 of the Charter states that the purposes and principles are:

> To maintain international peace and security, and to that end to take effective collective measures for the prevention and removal of threats to the peace, and for the suppression of acts of aggression or other breaches of the peace, and to bring about by peaceful means, and in conformity with the principles of justice and international law, adjustment or settlement of international disputes or situations which might lead to a breach of the peace.

With a few changes of words, including the word "liberty" substituted for the word "peace," the organization might have had real worth:

> To maintain international liberty, and to that end to take effective collective measures for the prevention and removal of threats to the people's liberties, and for the suppression of acts of aggression or other breaches of the people's liberties, and to bring about, in conformity with the principles of justice and international law, adjustment or settlement of international disputes or situations which might lead to a breach of the people's liberty.

Of course, non-democracies would be opposed to initiating liberty into the cause of the U.N. Why would any international organization that has, as members, nations governed not by the will of their citizens but by the authoritarianism of their unelected leaders, choose liberty as their quest? Too many governments of the world will be out of business if their people are allowed a free, fair, and frequent vote. Liberty would be their death-knell. Their ambassadors to the U.N. would surely be directed to vote against it, and they would do so willingly since if they failed, their ride in the U.N. would be over.

Even if we should forget the inherent organizational outrageousness and even if we forget the corruptions of the organization, there are the murderous genocides in which the U.N. has been delinquent, either by procrastination or by doing nothing: Among them, Cambodia, Burundi, Rwanda, Congo, Lebanon, Somalia, Bosnia, Kosovo, Sudan's war between the North and South, and Iraq.

The U.N. is pacing in the aisle of history, with its chief activity being the clearing of its throat.

Upon resignation in 2004, U.S. Ambassador to the United Nations John Danforth joined Pat Moynihan and Jeane Kirkpatrick as he spoke about the impotence of the U.N., this time regarding the genocide in Darfur. He concluded his remarks of disappointment while standing outside the United Nations Building and saying, "Why have this building? What is it all about?"

Today as for so many days before today, the old cry of

"U.S. Out of the U.N. and the U.N. Out of the U.S." would no longer go anywhere.

But there is a way to make it all take care of itself by the United States forming a Nations of Liberty Alliance (NOLA), which would be an organization of democracies throughout the world. The Nations of Liberty Alliance would not take the place of the U.N. but be a parallel organization—temporarily. Any nation accepted as a democracy could join both the U.N. and NOLA just as any nation can be a member of the E.U. or ASEAN or NATO or the O.A.S. or the African Union, and other multi-national organizations, while still being a member of the U.N.

No nation would be accepted into membership of NOLA unless its citizens choose their own government and have all the foundations of a true democracy; an independent judiciary, a military answerable to the elected civilian government, freedom of speech, freedom of assembly, freedom of religion, freedom of the press, freedom of organization, freedom of association, freedom of political activities, and freedom of movement. If a member-nation later undergoes a coup or adopts a termination of the principles of democracy, its membership is automatically terminated. In addition, aspirant membership could be offered for new democracies still in transition, with full membership to those who have undergone a proven tradition of democracy.

This would be a prestigious membership for any nation to enjoy since there would be moral qualifications rather than the practically "any flag admitted" procedure of the U.N. (It should be noted that the common procedure is not adhered to by the U.N. when it comes to Taiwan, which is a democracy and simply kicked out to make a passageway in for the People's Republic of China.) With NOLA in existence, what prestige would there be to an organization that embraces dictatorships, even totalitarians as the U.N. does, in contrast to an organization whose membership denies unelected dictatorships and is open only to those nations whose citizens are free and, thus, choose their own governments?

In terms of organizational functions of NOLA, the alliance would have no veto-empowered nations. Its major purpose would be one of providing a true forum for the people of the world since its leaders would be elected. Although no one could be naive enough to think they would all be good leaders, as long as democracy is retained in member nations, there will always be another election in near time.

The NOLA Compact would be brief and direct without ambiguity: Recognizing that liberty is a birthright, NOLA would be formed to be dedicated to all peoples of the world having the ability to control their destiny through free, fair, and frequent elections of their governments while maintaining all the elements of liberty.

NOLA would not have a military, but it could borrow from a paraphrased and slightly changed Article 5 of NATO:

> The Parties agree that an armed attack of a non-democracy against one or more NOLA members shall be considered an attack against them all and consequently

they agree that, if such an armed attack occurs, each of them, in exercise of the right of individual or collective self-defense may assist the member or members so attacked by taking forthwith, individually or in concert with other members, such action as it deems necessary including the use of armed force, to restore and maintain the liberty of member nations.

If, in time, NOLA proves to be more effective than the U.N., the United States could then provide a higher budget to NOLA, not by taking more funds from the U.S. taxpayer, but by taking a commensurate amount of funds from what had been already budgeted for future appropriations to the U.N. As we continue to take more and more of our funds in a trade of organizational budgeting, NOLA nations could mandate that members no longer be a member of both organizations but should make a choice.

In truth, without the financial support of the United States, the U.N. would have little if any substantive or influential life.

There is currently no organization that represents the people of the world. Without such an organization, it could well be assumed that the people of the world are not considered to be as important as unelected leaders. That, in itself, is a many-decades mandate that we cannot permit to go continually unchallenged.

At this writing, next year, 2020, the United Nations organization will celebrate its 75th anniversary. One year after its founding, its first Secretary-General, Trygve Lie, praised that organization as "a fire-station ready with a hose on the world stage." At the time, that good man didn't know that the fire station would be controlled by arsonists, chiefly financed by those who lived in the best and ultimately the most endangered house in the neighborhood.

For those from other free nations, recognize that you, too, are targets of the worst of those who probably sit close to you at the U.N.

EPILOGUE

IT'S DONE.

IT'S OVER.

I so much wish those two sentences were in reference to this book rather than in reference to what I believe to be the most magnificent city on earth: Hong Kong.

But in terms of the book, I do believe the writing of it is close to done. It is the 8th of January 2020. Tomorrow Hong Kong people will either continue to be living in liberty as before—or living in servitude to please a master named Xi, and those are the two open options. (The reason I prefaced that sentence with "I believe" is because authors of non-fiction often don't know when a particular book they have been writing is done. I'm one of them.) I do know, however, what I will not do: I will not go on a tour of bookstores and radio and television shows to sell copies of the book. The reason I am not going to do that anymore for any book is because when I was a kid, my parents did not say, "When you grow up, we want you to be a beggar."

Something else happened. It was some five months after 2020 began: President Trump of the United States gave a speech on the 29th of May 2020 from the Rose Garden of the White House in which he courageously condemned the leading role of President Xi's release of a virus through nations of the world, causing hundreds of thousands of deaths. Regrettably he gave no indication of a U.S. recognition of Hong Kong as an independent entity with its own government maintaining the liberties in which Hong Kong people had already been living. Instead, new dictatorial orders were already flowing to Hong Kong people from the People's Republic of China's government in Beijing by the person of Xi Jinping.

This was the time, I believe, for a U.S. President (Trump) to act by vastly reducing diplomatic relations with the PRC and give consistent friendship to Hong Kong by introducing U.S. recognition of Hong Kong as a small and strong and independent democracy.

As the writer of this book, I am very grateful that you read *A Profile of Hong Kong*, which was started right after the leader of the People's Republic of China betrayed the

PRC's pledge to Great Britain which is specified in Chapters Five and Fifteen.

If I editorialized at times within this book, I am sorry.

GLOSSARY

BASIC LAW
The Mini-Constitution for Hong Kong established by the People's Republic of China, somewhat based on the Joint Declaration. (April 4, 1990)

BILL OF RIGHTS ORDINANCE
1991 Hong Kong local law based on the International Covenant on Civil and Political Rights (ICCPR) and the International Covenant on Economic, Social and Cultural Rights (ICESCR)

BLOC = BASIC LAW DRAFTING COMMITTEE
The committee that composed the Basic Law. There were 59 members, 36 from the PRC, 23 from Hong Kong. In the end, all decisions had to be approved by the PRC.

BDTC = BRITISH DEPENDENT TERRITORIES CITIZEN PASSPORT

Used by those living in Hong Kong for travel. Does not give the "right of abode" in Great Britain.

(BNO) BRITISH NATIONAL OVERSEAS PASSPORT

Authorized by Great Britain to replace all British Dependent Territories Citizen's DTC's by the 1st of July 1997. Does not give the "right of abode" in Great Britain.

BRITISH NATIONALITY (HONG KONG) ACT OF 1990

Gives 50,000 heads of households in Hong Kong the "right of abode" in Great Britain (with dependents, approximately 225,000 people.) The PRC said it would not recognize those passports.

CFA

A common reference to the Court of Final Appeal (pre-July the 1st of 1997 was in Great Britain. After the 1st of July 1997, it would be in the People's Republic of China.)

CPP OR CP

A common reference to the Communist Party

DISTRICT BOARDS

Provides a forum for public consultation in Hong Kong. Also provides some local recreational and cultural activities. 19 members.

EXCO = EXECUTIVE COUNCIL

Similar to a Cabinet. Five of its sixteen members must also be members of the Legislative Council.

GUANGDONG

The province surrounding Guangzhou

GUANGZHOU = CANTON

Using Pinyin spelling (see below) for the same city of Canton

HONG KONG ALLIANCE IN SUPPORT OF THE DEMOCRATIC AND PATRIOTIC MOVEMENT IN CHINA

A group, including Szeto Wah and Martin Lee, organized to support the students who demonstrated in Tiananmen Square in 1989 and has continued to protest human rights violations in China.

HONG KONG-MACAU WORKING GROUP

Advisory group appointed by the PRC. Xu Ze was the head of the Political Department.

JOINT DECLARATION ON THE FUTURE OF HONG KONG, SIGNED BY GREAT BRITAIN AND THE PEOPLE'S REPUBLIC OF CHINA

Establishing all of Hong Kong's transfer to the PRC on the 1st of July 1997 as a Special Administrative Region for 50 years under "one country, two systems." (Initialed on the 26th of September 1984 and signed on the 19th of

December 1984.) This is a big one as it is a further promise not kept by the PRC in 2019.

JLG = JOINT LIAISON GROUP (SINO-BRITISH)

The 26th of September 1984 through the 1st of January 2000 group of representatives of both Great Britain and the People's Republic of China meeting in Beijing, London, and Hong Kong at least once a year in each of the three locations for liaison and consultation without being an organ of power. Each side has a senior representative of Ambassadorial rank and four other members with a staff of 20. Their proceedings are confidential unless otherwise agreed by both sides.

LEGCO = LEGISLATIVE COUNCIL

Prior to the elections of 1985, all Legco members were appointed by the Governor. In 1985, the first indirect elections for 26 of the members to the Legco took place through functional constituencies and electors. In 1991 an addition was made of the first direct elections for 18 of its 60 seats. On the 17th of September 1995, for the first time, there was a fully elected Legco as a body of 60 with 20 elected by Geographical Constituencies, 30 elected by Functional Constituencies, and 10 by an Electoral College.

OMELCO = OFFICE OF MEMBERS OF THE EXECUTIVE AND LEGISLATIVE COUNCILS

Secretariat for members of both groups.

PAP

The People's Armed Police of the People's Republic of China, which is a paramilitary force under orders of the Communist Party's Central Military Commission.

PEKING = BEIJING

Same city. Peking was used pre-Pinyin, which was instituted in 1979. (See Below). Peiping had also been used prior to Pinyin.

PLA

The People's Liberation Army of the PRC.

PINYIN

New spelling and pronunciation for Chinese Mandarin, introduced by the PRC to the world in the 1960s but barely used then. It wasn't instituted until 1979. (As examples, Mao Tse-tung became Mao Zedong and Peiping and Peking became Beijing.)

PROVISIONAL LEGISLATURE

Interim body to be established by the PRC in July 1997, planned as likely to replace the currently elected Legislative Council.

PRC

The People's Republic of China

PWC = PRELIMINARY WORKING COMMITTEE

Closed at the end of 1995 which operated as a Shadow Government for the PRC and never recognized by Great Britain. Replaced with the Preparatory Committee for 1996-97.

PREPARATORY COMMITTEE

Establishment in January 1996 using PWG's recommendations and dealing with how Hong Kong will be run by the PRC. At that time, 150 people were to be appointed by the PRC, with approximately half its members Hong Kong residents. Of the candidates chosen then by the PRC for the Preparatory Committee, none were from Hong Kong's Democratic Party. Among its duties was to decide on the membership of the provisional legislature, arrange the post-takeover election of future legislators, and nominate a Selection Committee of 400 people, all approved by Beijing, and they would pick the first Chief Executive for Hong Kong under the PRC's rule with that appointment then scheduled for August 1996 to take effect on the 1st of July 1997.

REGIONAL COUNCIL

Providing local services to the New Territories. The counterpart of the Urban Council which is used for Hong Kong Island and Kowloon. 36 members.

RIGHT OF ABODE

The right to live in a particular country or territory. In Hong Kong, generally referred to as the right to live in Great Britain.

SAR = SPECIAL ADMINISTRATIVE REGION

To be the designation of Hong Kong by China as of the 1st of July 1997 and Macau as of the 20th of December 1997. It provides the basis of "one country, two systems."

SEZ = SPECIAL ECONOMIC ZONES

Chinese cities given special tax breaks. Shenzhen is the one closest to Hong Kong, and Zhuhai is the one next to Macau.

THE THREE TREATIES AS THE PRC CALLS THEM:

Treaty of Nanking (1842) = Hong Kong Island ceded in perpetuity to Great Britain.

The Convention of Peking (1860) = Kowloon and Stonecutters Island ceded in perpetuity to Great Britain.

The Second Convention of Peking (1898) = The New Territories leased to Great Britain for 99 years from the 1st of July 1898 through the 30th of June 1997.

Instead, sometimes the PRC uses the Shanghai Communique as a numbered treaty, sometimes as the third treaty. It isn't a treaty at all but was a document stating U.S. views and the PRC's views and defined that way within the document. Some of the views were in agreement with the other side, and some were in disagreement with the other side.

URBAN COUNCIL
Providing local, municipal services in urban areas of Hong Kong Island and Kowloon. (Garbage collection, parks maintenance, recreation, and culture, etc.) 40 Councilors.

XIANG GANG
Title for Pinyin (see above) for Hong Kong and used after the takeover.

ANOTHER NOTE TO THE
READER FROM THE AUTHOR

But not very sorry.

What you have read is, of course, a book—but Hong Kong itself was filled with flesh and breath, with lives, with so many of those lives still holding memories that remain golden and kind and loving and free and what the entire world should be and can be and, in hope, what will be.

Many of those who are currently being taken through the streets to Beijing are being sent to be "tried" for "crimes" against Xi Jinping's demands while in truth, those to be tried are the angels of our times as Hong Kong people wanting to retain freedom from birth forward and who have lived in freedom in Hong Kong and who cherish future liberties for all Hong Kong people and for all those who want to join them in being free without fear of freedoms of liberty ever being taken away again.